What is Really Going On?

BOOKS BY KEITH HILL

NON-FICTION
The New Mysticism
The God Revolution
Striving To Be Human

CHANNELLED
Experimental Spirituality
Practical Spirituality
Psychological Spirituality
What Is Really Going On?
Where Do I Go When I Meditate?
How Did I End Up Here?

POETRY
The Ecstasy of Cabeza de Vaca
Psalms of Exile and Return
The Bhagavad Gita: A New Poetic Version
Interpretations of Desire:
Mystical Love Poems by the Sufi Master Ibn 'Arabi
I Cannot Live Without You:
Selected Poetry of Mirabai and Kabir
Out of the Way World Here Comes Humanity!
The Lounging Lizard Poet of the Floating World

FICTION
Puck of the Starways
Blue Kisses

WITH PETER CALVERT
The Kosmic Web
Learning Who You Are
The Matapaua Conversations

What Is Really Going On?

Keith Hill

attar‖books

First published in 2015 by Attar Books
Auckland, New Zealand

Paperback ISBN 978-0-473-31817-8
Ebook ISBN 978-0-473-31818-5

Cover designed by Demonza

Attar Books is a New Zealand publisher which focuses on work that explores today's spiritual experiences, culture, concepts and practices. For more information visit our website:

www.attarbooks.com   www.keithhillauthor.com

Contents

What is going on *here*?

This is a channelled text. Since Jane Roberts started channelling Seth in the early 1960s, channelling has become common. However, for years I was sceptical. My spiritual training was in the psychospiritual teachings of Sufism and G.I. Gurdjieff's Fourth Way. Channelling wasn't on their curriculum. As a result, while I saw channelled books in bookshops, including by Roberts and Seth, I never paid any attention. In fact, I had a bias against them: I saw channelling as a fringe activity not worthy of my attention. Two encounters changed my mind.

First, I met Peter Calvert, a meditator. I was so impressed by his first channelled book, *Agape and the Hierarchy of Love*, that I offered to edit his second, *Guided Healing*. The material Peter was accessing was fresh and innovative, presenting metaphysical concepts in a way that was tuned to contemporary psychological, scientific and cultural thinking. This led me to reevaluate my prejudices. Searching online brought me to the Michael Teachings. These immediately resonated, because they were built on the foundations of Gurdjieff's Fourth Way teaching, but took it much further, particularly by adding reincarnation into the mix. Encountering the Michael Teachings was the second event that induced me to reverse my negative stance on channelling.

This turnaround led me to see my newly formed friendship with Peter Calvert as an opportunity. On the basis of the material he was channelling, Peter appeared to be communicating with a sophisticated non-embodied spiritual identity who had a penchant for explaining spiritual realities and processes in illuminating ways. If this was the case, I had a few questions of my own! Such as how the universe came into existence via the big bang, what preceded that event, how the physical and the spiritual are connected, what precisely is consciousness, how consciousness attaches to a body ... you get the picture. Armed with my questions—which soon added up to a total of one hundred—Peter carried out a series of short retreats at a beach in Matapaua, on New Zealand's Coromandel coast, where he channelled answers that astonished us both with the richness of their detail. These answers, along with a diary Peter kept during his retreats, became our first collaborative book, *The Matapaua Conversations*.

After spending two years processing the Michael Teachings, I next had the idea of clarifying my new understanding by writing it up. I worked on two books, but neither was satisfactory. I kept feeling something was missing. Then one day, totally unexpectedly, the following words came into my mind:

> This book begins with a warning. Becoming spiritual is not easy. Learning what your personal life plan is, understanding what you are here to achieve during the course of this particular lifetime, and deciding how to live in order to best give expression to your deepest spiritual aims, is no easily accomplished task.
>
> There are many barriers to understanding who you are and how you function as an individual. There are further barriers to putting hard won understanding into action in daily living. Some of these barriers are external, consisting of socially and religiously constructed taboos regarding what you may legitimately delve into. One is projected fear, which is a control mechanism that stops you entering deeply into yourself. If you are reading this, we can assume you have already overcome the majority of these external barriers.

Whoa! That wasn't me! The perspective wasn't mine, the tone wasn't mine. The words hadn't come from the person I knew myself to be. They had come from somewhere else. What had happened was that words had appeared in my mind, and I had written them down. I realised I was channelling! Whatever I was communicating with said it was human, but no longer needed to incarnate in human bodily form. It was a multi-faceted entity consisting of almost a thousand individuals who had completed their cycles of human incarnation. As they were no longer incarnated human beings, they preferred not to have a human name. For convenience, I simply call them "the guides".

This, then, is what is going on here, in this book. I am communicating with an identity that is a composite of hundreds of individuals who were formerly human beings. Our communication largely consists of me asking questions and the guides giving answers. Often those answers are expansive, going far beyond what I conceived when originally framing the questions. All this has led to me collaborating with Peter Calvert on more books. And we have each channelled further texts on our own.

This book, *What Is Really Going On?*, is the first in *The Channelled Q+A Series*. The series is designed to offer introductory ideas, with each book structured around twenty-one questions and questions. The guides encouraged me to canvas friends and friends of friends to gather a variety of questions that reflect common concerns about being human and living in the twenty-first century. The series currently consists of three books that present the guides' thoughts on spiritual matters in an easy-to-read format. Each book has a central theme—reincarnation in this book, meditation in *Where Do I Go When I Meditate?*, and life plans and self-enquiry in *How Did I End Up Here?* However, each also includes many unrelated questions on topics people find puzzling.

Regarding the channelling process, no hocus pocus is involved. I don't carry out any preparatory rituals. And while channelling I don't feel transported anywhere. I don't see visions or hear voices. Instead, it is a calm process that feels very normal. I put myself into a quiet inner state and wait to sense the presence of the guides. Often we make appointments, so when I am ready to transcribe their thoughts the guides are present. In my mind I tell them I am ready, ask a question, and a subtle stream of thoughts flows into my mind. The process can be likened to having a silent telephone conversation with people you don't see. Except instead of words in my ear I sense thoughts in my mind, which I write down as they arrive. All this occurs in my usual writing work space, at my keyboard, in front of my computer.

In stating this, I need to make clear what this book isn't. Because the questioners aren't face-to-face with the guides, the questions are necessarily general rather than personal. So this isn't a spiritual agony aunt column in which ethereal whoevers discuss highly personal problems. This is not close encounters of the confessional kind. But the agony aunt analogy is relevant. In a very straightforward sense, the guides "up there" draw on their personal experiences and understanding to clarify what is happening to us "down here." I hope readers find the contributor's questions, and the guides' replies, as illuminating as I have.

A big thank you to everyone who sent in their questions. Now let's get on with it.

Question 1

How come we're all so confused?

If each of us is a spirit living in a body, how come we know so little about what is going on? People tell so many different stories about what we are as spiritual beings, what the purpose of our life is, where we came from and where we are going. It's a babble of contradictory stories. Why are we all so confused?

THE GUIDES RESPOND:

We'll start by introducing ourselves. We're spiritual beings like you. Except we don't have a body. But we did in the past, many times.

We have repeatedly lived through the experience of occupying a human body and dealing with all the exciting, boring, wondrous and excruciating experiences that go with being human. We have been men, women, gay, indifferent to sex. We have been delirious with joy. We have suffered unimaginable pain. We have given birth. We have raised children. We have lost children. We have been slaves. We have been masters. We have oppressed. We have fought against oppression. We have escaped oppression. We have been caught and punished for daring to dream we could have freedom. We have had it all. We have had everything taken from us. We have experienced everything possible within the human field of experience. That is the experiential basis for our claim to authority on what you're living through that is called the human condition. We know because we've done it all.

Our claim to any kind of spiritual authority—we use the term *spiritual authority* in a special sense that we'll come back to shortly—is that we have completed our allotted time on the planet you still call home. We now view human existence from a more detached perspective, in what is generally but not quite accurately called the spiritual realm. Like you, during our time of human living we experienced daily dramas up close and personal. Like you we viewed many things as terribly important that now, when we look back, we can see weren't really of much significance at all. But that's just the deal when anyone lives a human existence. When you're walking through the forest it's impossible to see the forest as a whole. All you can see are trees. But now, detached and free, we do see the whole forest. We have a complete overview of the human situation. And this perspective is what, in this strictly limited sense, gives us may be said to be our spiritual authority.

The fact that you become lost in daily life, that you can't see beyond your immediate experience, was described poetically by Paul of Tarsus many years ago when he wrote "I see through a glass darkly." The fact is living life is necessarily up close and personal. It means feeling every touch on your skin, every blow to your heart, every stimulus in your groin, responding immediately and directly to whatever daily life throws at you, from eating breakfast, organising the kids for school, negotiating traffic lights on your way to work, dealing with upset clients, being pressured by managers, feeling the stress of meeting a deadline, and so on. Given that all this is the stuff of human life, that so much demands your attention minute by minute, it's no wonder that when you attempt to step back and gain an overview on what is going on you feel, like Paul, that you see through a glass darkly. How could it be otherwise?

Another analogy will indicate why this is so. Imagine you're a kid in a fun fair. There's such exciting stuff to do. There's the roller coaster to ride, the ghost train where you can scream in the dark, the coconut shy to throw balls at, candy floss, toffee apples and hot dogs to wolf down. And of course you're not there by yourself. You're with your family, maybe a bunch of friends. A huge part of the pleasure of being at the fun fair is sharing the experience with those you care about.

On the other hand, many factors make your presence at the fun fair possible, factors that you're not aware of at all. One is that whenever you want to go on a ride with your friends, or you feel hungry, you put out your hand and ask your parents for money to pay for it. For a kid money is a mysterious lubricant that your parents keep in their wallets or pockets that makes all your fun possible. Kids don't know what an effort parents have made to earn the money to ensure their kids can have a great time. Kids can't know because it's beyond their experience.

Then there's the fact that the fun fair isn't always fun. The ice cream may fall off your cone. Your friends might start making fun of you. You can lose contact with your parents and get lost. That kid in your class who really doesn't like you could turn up and say the nastiest things. Bullies might threaten to beat you up and steal the money your parents gave you to spend on rides.

All these positive, not understood, and negative factors are mixed up in your experience of the fun fair.

Of course, the analogy is that the fun fair is your life. When you're a child life is this mysterious experience in which things are organised for you and you're required to turn up and do as you're told. For an adult life is a very different experience. Adults are responsible for themselves and often also for others. They have to organise, pay their way, and are responsible when things don't turn out as expected, when things go sour. Adults pay the price for failure.

Yet—and here we arrive at a central issue, and why this first question is so often asked—while adults have to take on all these responsibilities, they often feel as clueless as children as to what is really going on. To return to our analogy, what *does* go on behind the scenes at the fun fair?

If it's a travelling fun fair, a lot of organising has occurred even before it arrives in town. Schedules are locked down months, even years, beforehand. Workers are signed up to transport equipment and to set up the tents, machinery, fencing, ticketing offices, and signs. New rides are commissioned, old rides have maintenance done on them. People are trained to perform the myriad tasks that keep the fun fair operating on time and in accordance with safety regulations.

The same happens with life. There is a lot of behind-the-scenes organising. Those living their life are in the same situation as children at the fun fair. They don't see what it has taken to get their experiences up and running. They don't comprehend what it has taken to initiate the ride that is their life.

What it takes to create the conditions within which anyone lives their life is actually very complex. Just as you can't describe to anyone in one sentence, or even one page, what it takes to get a fun fair up and running, so it is impossible to say in one sentence, or one page, what it takes to gets an individual life up and running.

To indicate just one mitigating factor, no life occurs in isolation. Throughout your lifetime you interact significantly with at least a dozen, maybe several dozen, people. Just as fun fair rides are not there by accident but have been designed, built and put into place, so each significant "ride" you have with other people during your life has been planned and designed and the conditions in which you both may meet have been prepared. Significant interactions are very rarely random.

Then consider the extent to which each of your friends (and enemies) interact with dozens of others who are significant to them. And how there are billions of interlinked individual human beings currently living on this planet. To explain the intricacies of all those interactions is scarcely an easy matter. Yet—and here we hope we are not, as the saying goes, biting off more than we can chew—what we undertake to do in this book is to clarify the most important facets that make possible what you experience as "the ride of your life."

In relation to this Paul made another statement: "When I was a child, I spoke as a child, I understood as a child, I thought as a child; but when I became a man I put away childish things." Some of your most cherished thoughts, the notions you cling to to help you explain your life to yourself, are in fact no more than childish things. A major contributor to your confusion about what is happening to you and others you love is that you cling to ideas, feelings and explanations that confuse rather than clarify. In order to perceive with clarity, in order to replace confusion with understanding, in order to grow from spiritual child to spiritual adult, you need to put away childish things.

In what follows we aim to clarify and illuminate, little by little, so your understanding may grow from childish to adult. And the first notion we need to introduce in order to dispel a fundamental layer of confusion that definitely darkens the glass through which you perceive your life is that of reincarnation. Appreciating the role reincarnation plays in your life is basic to understanding what is going on.

Reincarnation? Yeah, right!

If reincarnation is a really existing process, what's its purpose? If I've been here before, how come I don't really and deeply know that I'm doing the right thing with my life? The thing is, I don't even know if it matters what I do! And, to be frank, dealing with just this one life is difficult enough without bringing past lives into the picture.

THE GUIDES RESPOND:

An appreciation of the fact of reincarnation is necessary to achieve a deep understanding about what is going on in your life. That is, if you seriously do want to shatter the childish notions that ensure you remain confused and see only "through a glass darkly."

But before reviewing how reincarnation impacts on your life we need to discuss why there is such resistance to the notion of reincarnation in the first place. Such resistance is entirely the creation of cultural conditioning. For anyone born in the East, and particularly raised as a Buddhist or in one of the Indian dharmas, the notion of reincarnation is fed to them in their mother's milk, as the saying goes. Their cultural conditioning is entirely in favour of reincarnation, even if many quite false ideas are tagged to their notion of what reincarnation involves. Nonetheless, for them our proposal that reincarnation is a central fact of human existence would not be a stumbling block at all.

Historically, in the West, many groups have in fact accepted and taught reincarnation. These include ancient Greek philosophers, the Druids, the Norse Vikings, and a number of Jewish and Christian groups. However, we are not here to provide a history lesson. We are here to tell you how it is. Or, at least, how human existence is from our spiritual perspective.

The basic fact is that anyone reading this book has been here before. Many times, in fact. When we used the analogy of the fun fair and raised the issue of what happens behind the scenes so the fun fair may arrive in town and function successfully, we were referring to the mechanism of reincarnation. Ignoring for now the mechanics of how spirit and matter interact (we'll come back to that another time) the process of reincarnation is, in effect, the oil that makes the machinery of human existence run.

What is the purpose of reincarnation? It is the same as your existence as a spiritual being: to generate favourable life conditions by which you may experience, learn and grow.

In this sense the process of living everyday human existence and your process as a spiritual being is the same. Every child goes through the process of learning to crawl, to walk, to talk, how go to the toilet, and how to interact acceptably with others. Every child goes to school to learn practical, creative, social and intellectual skills, the aim being that they may eventually take their place as an adult who acts responsibly in the wider human world. This exact same process is reflected in the spiritual dimension. In fact, the socialisation of a child from naive and unskilled to experienced, knowing and self-reliant, who is also able to feel compassionately for others, is directly reflected on the spiritual level.

Every spiritual identity begins its existence as naive, unskilled and unknowing. Every spiritual identity initially lacks the inner depth needed to appreciate and sympathise with what others around them are going through. Why can't a child appreciate what adults around them are feeling and thinking? Simply, they lack adult experience.

Each child progresses through a variety of experiences, from childhood to teen to adult, which happens naturally as they age. As individuals graduate from the education system and enter the workforce they inevitably interact with a range of other people. Some they lock horns with, others they enjoy playing with, yet others they work happily or unhappily with. In the process everyone learns about themselves and others. This is the normal progression of human learning. The key to learning, however, is not memorising facts or passing exams. The key to learning is having a range of diverse experiences and drawing lessons from them.

Sports people talk about what they draw from each game as "learnings." Each and every time they are on the field they perform some plays well, other plays poorly, act out their part in a brilliant move and maybe ruin another move with a basic error. After each game they analyse what they did well and what they didn't. They figure out how to repeat the excellent parts of their performances, how to correct badly performed skills, and how to improve on-field decision-making. Their takeaway, what they process from each game, constitutes their learnings. Learnings are basic to developing one's skills and talent and becoming a better sports person.

Exactly the same process applies to you when you enter the field of life, given that each time you are born is like a new game you start to play. Of course, the difference between reincarnation and a normal sports game is that the aim of being born and entering the game of life is not to win, but rather to perform as well as you can.

Let's put this into a developmental context. Do you expect children to run the first day they get to their feet? Of course not. At first the child stands, wobbles, falls. Only after many attempts does the child learn how to walk. And only years later, after physically growing, and after much concerted application and practice, is the child able to take part in games like football, tennis, horse-jumping, archery.

Similarly, no spiritual identity when first born into a human body suddenly becomes Mozart or Gandhi or Marie Curie. It takes many repeated experiences, from which different kinds of learnings are derived, to develop from naive and unskilled to talented and able. Reincarnation facilitates this progression. Reincarnation provides the opportunity to repeatedly enter the field and fray of human existence, to try things out, to correct errors, and to enhance what you are already good at, all so you may develop your potential to its maximum. An individual only becomes a Mozart, a Gandhi or a Marie Curie after working hard to achieve that level of expertise.

This, in a nutshell, is the purpose of reincarnation. It provides a mechanism by which naive and inexperienced spiritual identities may learn to become skilled, knowing and loving.

In stating this we are aware it assumes two ideas that may never have occurred to you. The first is that you, as a spiritual identity, are not static. Every experience you undergo contributes to your growth. Just as a human child grows into a human adult, and the ability of the adult depends on what it has learnt from its experiences, so your growth as a spiritual identity depends on what you experience and what you learn from your experiences.

Just as the human world acknowledges those who apply themselves and make more of themselves than who, what or where they were previously, so the spiritual world acknowledges those who use their experiences to make themselves more than they were. The difference is that in the human world acknowledgement generally takes the form of social status or monetary rewards, whereas in the spiritual realm acknowledgement consists of you appreciating that you are making the most of your opportunities, you are becoming all you have the potential to be and then sharing what you learn with others.

This is the situation we, currently playing the role of spiritual advisors, now find ourselves in. We have collectively undergone innumerable lives, we have drawn many subtle and insightful "learnings" from our experiences, and we now direct what we have gained from the entire process back to you, to offer you insights regarding what you are going through.

Thus reincarnation, far from being weird and strange, is just another aspect of a developmental process you are already engaged in, whether you realise it or not. Each day, should you wish to take advantage of the opportunity, you can process what has happened to you, review how you reacted to others, consider how others reacted to you, dig into the times you performed poorly, recognise what you did well, and decide what you wish to repeat to develop to a higher level, or alternatively what you wish to knock on the head and eliminate from your daily routines. This option to develop yourself is available to you today, tomorrow and every single day after that.

On the sports field the same developmental process occurs game by game, sometimes even play by play. It consists of performing, reviewing, learning, and trying again, all while attempting to do things differently and to perform better. For you as a spirit residing in a human body, this process occurs not just day by day, decade by decade, but also, we are asserting, life by life.

The purpose of human existence is to develop skills, to learn from experiences, to become knowledgeable, to become loving, to share, to form goals, to work together to achieve goals, to accomplish, to make the world in which you live better. The same purpose applies in the spiritual realm.

Which brings us to the second major point about reincarnation. The human realm is actually an extension of the spiritual realm. The two are not separate. You are a spirit living in a human body. So whether you acknowledge it or not, you are already functioning on the spiritual plane. The spiritual is not somewhere else. It is right here. In you. You are spiritual. It's just, as Paul said, you see through a glass darkly. So you don't perceive things as they are. And that is why you are confused.

Question 3

Then why can't I remember my past lives?

The way you explain reincarnation makes it sound very reasonable, even sensible. But how do I know the whole thing isn't baloney? Where's the evidence for reincarnation? Let's face it, a child at the fun fair and a sports person remember what they did last year, yesterday, a few minutes before. But we don't emerge from the womb remembering prior lives. It's all a mystery to us. So why don't we remember our past lives?

THE GUIDES RESPOND:

We will begin answering this question with the observation that forgetfulness is an absolutely necessary psychological factor in human life. Why?

Imagine you could remember, vividly and with the same impact with which they occurred, all those times you felt humiliated, slighted, insignificant. Imagine you could remember every single time you were in pain, every occasion you messed up, each instant you felt guilty or ashamed. What would happen if every single such moment came flooding back into your awareness simultaneously? Given you felt badly enough when each single event occurred, how terrible would you feel when the memory of them all came flooding back at once?

At best you would collapse under the impact of the psychological pain. At worst you would go mad, perhaps even kill yourself, due to being unable to cope with the pressure of feeling once again all those times in the past when you messed up, when things went wrong, when you were victimised, hassled, blamed.

Imagine the same occurring with all the happy times in your life. Imagine you could simultaneously remember all your best feelings, the times you screamed with laughter, the ecstasy of loving and feeling loved, the moments when you looked at a landscape, or the night sky, or another person, and felt overwhelmed by the wonder and mystery of it all. Imagine you re-experienced all those best feelings and thoughts at the same time. How would you function? How would you fulfil the requirements of your daily routines? As with the painful memories, you would be overwhelmed by a cacophony of overlapping impressions. And you would inevitably sag under the sheer weight of all those profound impressions and feelings.

In each case, with your awareness overwhelmed by painful or ecstatic feelings, how would you prepare breakfast, get the kids to school, travel to work, back the car into a parking spot, or deal with all the difficult and mundane problems of the day? You wouldn't be able to do it. You would either be too traumatised or too carried away to function at all in your normally effective manner.

Those who are unable to forget just one major past event in their life, such as losing a spouse or a child, are often rendered incapable of living a normal life. It can take years to overcome the emotional impact of loss and begin to function normally. Many never do return to normal. Now imagine the impact of every single major emotional event being remembered simultaneously. How could anyone cope? They couldn't. Psychologically, they would be torn in multiple directions at once.

The medical profession has a term for the condition that would result. It is schizophrenia. Schizophrenia is diagnosed as an inability to function in everyday reality, of being overwhelmed by imaginary voices and feelings. As far as anyone from outside was concerned, when they observed another person overwhelmed by memories and feelings originating in the past, they would observe them as lost in an inner world, hearing voices, responding to feelings, answering thoughts quite unrelated to the present moment. And they would be right. Such a person would be lost in the past and dissociated from the present. They would be in total schizophrenic meltdown.

We have dwelt at such great length on this in an attempt to show you what would happen to you if you were unable to forget, if you couldn't slip away from all your childhood pleasures and pains, if traumatic and ecstatic events remained undiminished and continuously present in your awareness. You would go mad. This is why forgetfulness is a human psychological necessity. Without forgetfulness no one could function at all.

This brings us to the nature of human awareness. By way of analogy, it could be said that human awareness is like a wave. You live constantly on the crest of the wave. The wave itself consists of multiple impressions. Most impressions are received via your senses and from the immediate world around you. Some impressions are echoes of what happened to you in the recent or distant past. These echoes trail off, some quickly, some slowly. Some impressions, such as being fired, or proposing marriage, may echo for weeks, months, or years.

This wave of impressions tends to have a very short lead-in and a long trailing wake. The height of the wave rises and falls depending on the intensity of the experiences you are undergoing. In addition, some waves are choppy because they are impacted by other people's waves, while some waves are simple and pure, containing only a single source of impressions.

Those whose awareness is overwhelmed by a past event have turned away from the incoming impressions and instead face backwards, towards the past. Their attention is focused on the emotional turbulence still churning in the trailing wake. These poor individuals are actually in a pathological state, which is usually diagnosed as grief, depression or some kind of disassociation. Usually it is treated with drugs. But, in fact, it is caused by an inability to separate from and to release past traumas. In these situations one needs to face up to what has happened, process it, resolve the hurt, and move on. Psychologically, release involves inwardly letting go of past impressions, turning around to face new incoming impressions, and once again functioning as is normal for that individual.

It needs to be noted that the same backward-turning of attention can also apply to pleasures. This is especially the case with sexual fetishes. In such a case a person has an intensely pleasurable sexual experience, usually when young, perhaps even before puberty, and it makes such an impression that this individual repeatedly attempts to recreate that feeling throughout their life. The fetish reflects the original impression, whether it involves gloves, or a nurse's uniform, or is associated with some particular texture or smell. In such a case the individual faces the incoming impressions, but lays past impressions over it, attempting to manipulate the new impressions so they echo the original intoxicating impressions.

Most people sit on the crest of their wave of awareness quite naturally, without clinging to past trauma and ecstasies. Impressions arrive, pass through them, then trail off into the past and are naturally forgotten. But from time to time everyone also finds that certain impressions become caught up inside them and don't trail away. In these cases they need to consciously process their impressions and find a way to absorb their impact before they can be let go and join all the other impressions that trail off into the functionally forgotten past.

With this somewhat extended introduction completed, we can now address the question of why you can't remember your past lives. There are two levels of answer.

The first is that you can't cope with the memory all that has happened to you in this life. So how much less could you cope with remembering everything that has happened to you in all your prior lives? If all the memories of what you felt in this current life would send you spinning into schizophrenia, imagine what would happen if you magnified that one hundred, three hundred, five hundred-fold? If everyone remembered just a tenth of what they felt and thought during all their prior lives the Earth would be populated by screeching, heaving lunatics.

The second answer is that in order to approach each life as a new opportunity you need to have a fresh start unencumbered by past errors and successes. To return to the earlier example of sport, when a player is on the field he or she needs to forget the error they just made, or the winning move to which they just contributed, and deal with the next play that develops in front of them, responding unencumbered by thoughts of failure or feelings of doing well.

In exactly the same way a newly-born individual needs to embark on "the ride of their life" unencumbered by prior successes and failures. This new life is a new opportunity for living and learning. Being overlaid with memories of past life experiences would impede, not assist, the playing out of this new opportunity.

Of course, establishing the conditions for a new life is much more complicated than this. You have developed skills in prior lives that naturally surface in this one. You have innate abilities and propensities. You naturally go towards certain experiences and avoid others. But these underlying conditions tend to be hidden from you. They sit unnoticed among all the other things you have forgotten you experienced over the course of your many prior lives.

And this, we assert, is as it should be. Forgetfulness is a necessary prerequisite for human existence. Not remembering past lives is a needed preliminary for experiencing this current life as immediate and fresh. Forgetfulness keeps you balanced and sane. Relatively speaking, of course.

Question 4

But where's the evidence
I've lived before?

Ok, what you said about forgetfulness makes sense. But here's the thing—I also wouldn't remember past lives if I had never had them. Maybe if I had some solid evidence I might be more inclined to accept the possibility of reincarnation. But right now I can't see that you've offered definitive evidence to support what you're saying. So where's the definitive evidence that I've lived before?

THE GUIDES RESPOND:

Definitive evidence would certainly be ideal. But is this a realistic request? Scientific predictions are based on probabilities, not on certainties. Science considers no explanation is final and definitive. Current explanations are always being tested and adjusted. There is acknowledgement that much in reality is intangible. Why? Because no one knows everything! And we include ourselves in that statement.

Experientially, your life is full of intangibles. You love your family and are loved in turn. But will this always be the case? Maybe. Maybe not. The world around you tells you you have to plan for retirement, that you need financial plans in place. But what definitive evidence do you have that you will reach retirement age? How do you know what your situation will be at that stage in your life? The world changes. Your body changes. Your circumstances change. You change. Of course, throughout your life you *do* have to make future plans. But you do so knowing in the back of your mind that everything could change. You make plans on the back of intangibles.

The problem arises when people turn intangibles into assumptions, then make those assumptions certainties. They live assuming that what they want to happen, what they have planned to happen, will indeed happen. Then when they reach the time when their plans should unfold and their plans don't, they are left stupified. They may feel their entire life is coming apart at the seams. What is really coming apart is that the assumptions they wove into their life are revealed as having been probabilities, not certainties. And the dice of probability didn't roll in their favour.

So this is one fundamental issue about finding definitive evidence: you live according to intangibles, not definites. The very nature of your existence, the question of where you were before you were born, where you will go after you die, your relationship to other people you love dearly, how you ended up in the life situation you are in ... you have no definite knowledge about any of this. It is all intangible.

This doesn't mean that nothing definite is the case. It just means that human perception is narrow, the human mind can't process huge amounts of data or deep information at once, and so key aspects of human existence, key aspects of what we earlier called the machinery of the fun fair, remains unknown to you. This isn't to say anything deliberately mysterious or to belittle your attempts to understand yourself and your life. This is just a statement of fact.

A second fundamental issue that impacts on your request for definitive evidence is psychological. Even when people are provided with clear evidence they often have great difficulty accepting that it exists, let alone process it and extract a plausible conclusion. This is the case today with human-caused climate change. Many people still want to deny the clear scientific evidence. Why?

Human psychological make-up is complex, so there are many reasons people refuse to accept the same evidence that others see as clear-cut. A fear of change is a significant factor. A desire to cling to what they currently have is another. Some invest their professional lives, their social identity, in a certain perspective. When evidence appears that contradicts that perspective they fight back, rejecting or even actively suppressing the evidence. Pig-headedness, a desire to be contrary, a need to run with the majority, are all factors as to why people reject evidence that logically leads to them needing to adjust their outlook. In this context, evidence that flatly contradicts someone's current worldview has no chance of making any kind of impression but a negative one.

The point we are making is that accepting evidence is never just about the validity of the evidence. It is also about being willing to accept and openly evaluate evidence. So when the question is asked, "Where's the definitive evidence for reincarnation?" we have to ask in return: How seriously are you asking?

If you are presented with evidence, some of which may be strong while other evidence may be weak but suggestive, are you willing to evaluate it openly, without falling back onto assumptions? Are you prepared to draw the conclusions that the evidence logically leads to? And are you prepared to follow the consequences, which may require you to jettison long-held beliefs? Are you really willing to give up ideas you have invested in emotionally and psychologically, ideas that you consider are part of your identity?

Without a commitment from you to be open, to be willing to reevaluate your outlook and to change the way you view your own life, your question is not sufficiently serious to achieve a serious answer. Your question is, frankly, just hot air.

In stating this we don't mean to be insulting. We are just telling it how it is. This is what we intend to do in all these responses. We will answer seriously and with a loving intent. But we also require you to be open and willing to evaluate what we offer without being defensive or falling back onto long-held assumptions.

With this preamble over, we can move onto the issue of evidence for reincarnation. Three kinds of evidence are available.

The first consists of ancient testimony. This is provided in literature generated by Pythagorean and Platonic schools of philosophy, which viewed reincarnation as essential to human existence. Reincarnation was also widely accepted in ancient India, being written of in the Vedas, the Upanishads, and the *Bhagavad Gita*. Of course, reincarnation is basic to Buddhist teachings, with acceptance of reincarnation seen in practice in the selection of the Dalai Lama. The ancient Celts, led by Druid priests, also accepted reincarnation as real.

These ancient spiritual adventurers had varying ideas about the mechanism by which reincarnation occurred. This is understandable because every new idea, whether it is social, cultural, economic, scientific, or spiritual, gets adjusted over time as more contributors draw on what they have discovered to add to it and refine it. The result is that contradictory ideas are batted around in any field of human endeavour. This equally applies to reincarnation. However, as more people draw on their experiences and discoveries around reincarnation, its mechanism will become progressively clearer.

The second main source of evidence regarding reincarnation is in contemporary research. In particular Dr Ian Stevenson, based at the University of Virginia, initiated a two decade study of children's accounts of their prior lives. He put an emphasis on physical markings and phobias carried over from prior lives in an attempt to establish tangible evidence for reincarnation. He also collected verbal testimony from people about prior existences and sought to find evidence to confirm what they said. Naturally, Stevenson had—and still has—many critics, some of whom have chosen an extreme sceptical approach rather than an open one. As a result his findings remain controversial. Nonetheless, his studies, and other studies inspired by his work, offer an extremely useful source of data regarding reincarnation.

So for anyone seriously seeking evidence of reincarnation, these two sources are available. Of course, the first source, that of ancient texts, cannot be tested, so can neither be confirmed or denied. They just stand as a stimulus to further enquiry. Nonetheless, the fact that Greek, Indian and Celtic cultures each accepted reincarnation, and that the notion was sustained over an extended period of time – in the East for well over two thousand years – suggests on the one hand that acceptance of reincarnation may be totally and only socially conditioned, or that there is something to it. Either way, it needs to be openly considered. Yet clearly this source is not even suggestive, let alone decisive, for the sceptical.

The evidence supplied by Dr Ian Stevenson is more difficult to casually dismiss. He attempted to establish protocols and to test what people remembered against available facts. For those who seriously wish to investigate whether reincarnation does occur, Stevenson's case studies need to be considered.

However, both these sources are external to you. They may offer suggestive information, however from your perspective they are impersonal, abstract, even somewhat speculative. If the notion of reincarnation is to have any direct relevance to you it has to be personally obtained evidence, in the context of your own life. That is where we suggest the third and the most significant source of information in support of reincarnation is to be found: in the details of your own approach to life and living. Of course, to evaluate this evidence you need to put aside existing assumptions either for or against reincarnation and evaluate what you find openly and without bias.

In order to review how reincarnation has impacted on your life, we suggest you begin by evaluating your natural propensities and preferences. To do this you need to look intently at your behaviour and what motivates what you do and why you do it. Everyone has psychological patterns of propensities, that is, what you naturally like to do, and preferences, what you choose or are driven to do.

Clearly, some propensities and preferences are instilled in you by your family and your wider culture. You prefer to live in certain ways because that is how you were brought up or because that is what is available where you live. Some preferences are biological and genetic, as is seen in the ways that everyone tends to prefer the food they were raised to eat, food that also tends to accord with their body's genetic makeup. All these preferences we call biological and social givens. They are what is inherent in your body, in your immediate social environment, and in your culture.

But there are other preferences and propensities that are not strictly cultural, environmental or biological. We challenge you to examine what is most important in your life, what most deeply—and we mean very deeply—attracts you, what most profoundly sustains your deepest drives, and what consequently most visibly impacts on your life. They visibly impact in the sense that they drive you in your most important life goals. But don't look just in terms of social and practical manifestations. Look under, behind, and inside yourself to what drives you with the most intense intent. Then, once you have identified this (or these) deep level drives, see if you can discover where they come from.

It is important that you grasp what we are suggesting here. Being driven in the same way that one of your parents or dearest friends has been driven in their life isn't the drive we are asking you to discover. Imitating a parent or a peer, seeking their approval or striving to outdo them, striving to be the best, certainly does motivate people in their lives. But these are psychological factors that derive from your social interactions with others. These are not the drives we are talking about. The drives we ask you to ferret out are those that you likely rarely or never discuss with others, drives that you may not even admit to having. But they are drives that are deeply meaningful to you.

Identify these drives buried within yourself. Then ask where they come from. In proposing this we are not asking you how you have adjusted these deep drives to fit into the world around you. Nor how they result in you being rewarded or rejected by others. Nor the ways they make you happy or sad. Nor the ways they manifest in the world. What we ask you to consider is why do you have these drives? Why are they so important to you? Why do they exist at a level that is deepest within you? Why are they there at all?

It is likely you won't be able to say *why* you feel any particular deep drive is so important to you. Nor will you be able to say *where* it came from. Or *how* it came to be so significant to you. You only know that it is deeply present. We contend this is because it is a drive you brought with you into this life. But you don't, you can't, recognise this as being the case because, of course, you don't remember any previous lives, let alone the specific circumstances that gave rise to that drive. So you have no idea of how it came to exist in you.

Nonetheless, if you examine this drive intently you will come to see that, at a very deep level, you know that your life's satisfaction depends on you travelling in the direction it urges you to go. And that equally applies whether the journey is for good or for ill. By this we mean you may feel that following your deepest drive may lead to conflict, whether with others or within yourself, because it requires you to make a fundamental change in how your approach your life. Or you may perceive it leading to ends you cannot foresee. As a result, part of you has a bad feeling about it. Not because it is bad in itself, but because it will lead to change. And that in turn may generate worry, anxiety, even fear. Nonetheless, in your depths you know your deepest satisfaction depends on you responding to this drive, in letting it express itself in your life, in going where it takes you, whatever the consequence. To repeat, this is a drive that doesn't originate in your biology, social conditioning or inherited traits. This emanates from you, at your core. It reflects decisions made by you before this life, manifests in activities you chose before incarnation, and it pushes you to achieve goals you selected before you were born.

Significantly, what you have selected depends on what you have already done or not done in previous lives, which you now wish to follow through on by addressing, changing, developing, or shifting into another gear. In all this we are suggesting that in the deepest levels of your own self nothing is arbitrary. It is there because you put it there, because you decided this is what you wish to achieve, this is what you need to face up to, this is what you need to do to soar. The drive we ask you to identify is essential to all this occurring. It is an essential part of who, why, what and where you are.

We realise this could easily be viewed as yet another intangible, that in offering this exercise as "definitive evidence" of reincarnation we are not really doing any such thing. This is because in order to find evidence within the circumstances of your own life that what you have done previously is impacting on your current life, *you* need to do the digging. *You* need to find the data. *You* need to shift it for evidence. *You* need to convince yourself. No one else can do for you. As with seeking evidence that you are loved and love, no one else can convince you whether your love is real. Only you can do it by digging into what you feel, perceive and know. And no one else can do that digging for you. Only you.

This is why we have provided a practical exercise by which you may obtain, if not evidence definitive enough to convince anyone else, then at least material that will suggest to you that much more going on beneath the surface of the fun fair that is your life than you have previously been privy to. To offer a variant on the statement that introduced a television show popular in the 1990s, "the truth is *in* there." You just need to diligently seek it out.

If there's a big plan why is it so hush-hush?

I know I've made choices in life, such as selecting work, or when I've embraced or run away from a relationship, or when I've naturally been attracted to new people or new situations, and I've felt "this is the right thing for me to do." Even though at the time I didn't know why. So I see that I have deep drives. But if they are part of a bigger plan, why is it all so hush-hush? Why do I feel like I've been left out of what is happening at a deep level in my own life? Why haven't I been let in on the secret?

THE GUIDES RESPOND:

The question is asked, and we are assuming it is in the context of what we offered in the previous response, why do human beings have an individual life plan, a plan they formed for themselves before they were born, but now they are living their life it turns out they have no direct knowledge of what that plan is? Why is this so?

Our previous comments on forgetfulness equally apply in relation to your life plan. When you enter a new life, part of the pleasure is living it unencumbered by expectations. And here we explicitly refer to your own expectations. If you knew your own life plan, and then saw you were diverging from it, whether just a little or radically, a natural human reaction is to castigate yourself for doing so. Or, alternatively, to staunch it out and brazenly dare yourself to do the opposite of what is expected. And the mere fact that what is expected was generated not by others but by you, for your own benefit, would not lessen your desire to act contrary to your own plan.

These two characteristics, of castigating oneself, especially with feelings of guilt or unworthiness, or of doing the opposite of what is in one's own interests, are very common psychological traits. Self-castigation, of course, is often projected outwards, onto others, so they—whether "they" are identified in terms of sex, race, age, social status, wealth, poverty, being unwed, or being multiply wed—are privately or publicly blamed and shamed for being as they are. Similarly, a range of different motives, including revenge, spitefulness, willed ignorance, even a desire to protect others, lead individuals to do the opposite of what, at their deepest level, they actually wish to do.

Conflicts between these two levels, on the one hand the everyday psychological level, and on the other the deeper core consciousness level, a core human beings call spiritual, are what is at issue here.

You live at the everyday psychological level. This is where you are aware during your waking life. This is where you process experiences and where you feel, think and speak from. In contrast, the inner drives we refer to, and the plans behind those drives, exist at the level of your spiritual core consciousness. The reason you don't perceive your own plans, the reason you consider it to be a big secret, is due to the fact that you are not in direct contact with your own core consciousness. So in order for you to become aware of your own deep plans you need to shift your awareness from the everyday psychological level to that of your own core.

The issue then becomes, how do you do so? Clearly, if it was easy to do everyone would be doing it. And you wouldn't be asking this question. As we have just observed, the everyday psychological level of awareness contains various emotional and attitudinal traits, many of which are negative and keep your attention glued to what is happening immediately around you. Fear, self-pity, resentment, a desire to run away, a desire to confront, even fight, along with many others, are psychological traits that fill your awareness during your waking hours. Then, when people go to sleep at night, they are often still saying the things they meant to say, or still fighting the day's fight, in their dreams. So there is no space in their awareness for information emanating from their core consciousness, simply because their awareness is gummed up with everyday concerns.

To become open to information coming from your core consciousness you need to clear a space in your awareness. And doing that requires diminishing negative and limiting psychological traits. Guilt, resentment, self-castigation, blame, fears—they all have to go. Only after you acknowledge the existence of these traits, address them, and reduce their impact in your awareness, will you be able to access your own core consciousness, easily and whenever you wish.

Why access your own deep self? *Because it knows!* It knows what your plans are this time round. It knows why you have these particular drives and not others. It knows what you are trying to achieve. It knows why you face particular obstacles. It knows what the goal of your life is.

Having observed this, we need to add that behind all these questions is a feeling, a very common human feeling, that there is a big secret to life, and that if only you could talk to the right person, or to the right spiritual being, maybe to a deceased saint or to someone who is enlightened, or if you could even talk to God, or at least to one of God's representatives, you could be given a wink and a nudge, be initiated into the inner sanctum, and so learn all the "big secrets."

Let's be clear here. There are no "big secrets" knowing which will turn on the "big light" and illuminate your being so all your questions are answered. That isn't how reality works. However, there certainly exists what could be termed hidden knowledge. But this knowledge is hidden not because there is an inner circle of some kind protecting it. It is hidden because you are not yet in a position to access it. When you in such a position you will do so.

Much of the frustration people feel in spiritual circles is due to the fact that they are still inexperienced and naive. They are like children in the schoolyard, playing with the other kids. But really they want to be with the adults, taking part in adult talk and adult activities. But they can't, because they are still children.

How does a child join the adults? How does an inexperienced individual get to join those who are experienced? By applying themselves. By growing. You grow by undergoing a range of experiences and drawing life lessons from those experiences. Within everyone's trajectory through the full range of possible human experiences there is choice, there are self-selected goals, there are failures, there are repeated efforts, and there is success. This is inevitable in all learning and growing. You become better at being human by engaging again and again with chosen experiences and progressively doing a better, more knowing, more loving job.

One of these jobs, among many, many possible other tasks, is shifting your awareness from being entirely engaged with the social world at the everyday psychological level and opening it up so you can receive information from your core consciousness.

If you wish to learn about your life plan this time round, if you wish to dispel the uncertainty you feel when making key decisions, or if you just wish to know whether or not you are on track, we advise you to carry out the exercise described in the previous response. If you identify your deep drives, then the plan that led to those drives being formulated will also begin to come into focus for you. Meditation, quietening down your mind, and asking your deep self questions is also productive. The point is you need to hold back and quieten the everyday psychological level buzz of thoughts and emotions that normally fill your awareness. Put it all to one side so that the subtle voice of your deep self may be heard. Practise diligently and it will come through!

As a final remark, we need to further clarify the point we made about the difference between child and adult. We intended to comment on people feeling frustrated and impatient. You may look around and feel that others "have it together" much more than you do. This applies as much in the spiritual sphere of human interactions as to any other human activity. Our observation that some individuals are naive and inexperienced and others are experienced, and that this differentiates children from adults on the spiritual level, is technically correct. However, the reality is more complex than this.

One key factor is that people usually have no idea where they stand on the child-adult continuum. They are quite unable to evaluate how spiritual they and others are. It is also the case that some individuals have taken on an overtly spiritually-oriented task in this life as part of a multi-life goal. So they outwardly appear to be more spiritual than you. However, this is not necessarily the case. You may actually be more spiritually experienced than them, but this time round you have taken on more overtly mundane tasks, again as part of a specific multi-life goal. So in this life you are, as the saying goes, hiding your light under a bushel. The fact that you are drawn to a book such as this indicates that your deep self certainly is having significant impact on your life, even if you aren't so sure.

So we would make two pertinent observations. The first is that who is spiritually a child, who a teen, and who an adult is not as clear-cut as might appear. To differentiate you need to see individuals as entirely spiritual identities, free of their body. Because this won't occur until everyone's bodies have died, including your own, this is a comparison you are currently unable to make. Then, when you are in a disembodied state, it is a comparison it won't occur to you to make, because relative status is of zero concern in the spiritual realm, and anyway you will be engaged in far more interesting activities.

The second observation is that there is actually no point in comparing during your incarnation in this earthly realm. You are on your personal multi-life trajectory, during which you are choosing particular experiences from the emporium of all available human experiences.

Others are on their personal trajectory, selecting experiences that attract them. Comparing, especially comparing to make yourself feel small, lesser or inadequate, is counter-productive. It just adds another layer of opaqueness to the dark glass of your perception.

Growth necessarily requires that some are children, some are teens, and some are adult. No one can become an adult without first being a child. Everyone has been, is, or will be, one of these three. So relax. It's all part of the magic of experiencing the fun fair. Embrace the moments! Play with all you have! This is the ride of your life!

I feel so dumb. Don't I need a teacher or guru?

You said people grow spiritually from child through teen to adult. If we feel we're beginners how should we progress? Should we be seeking out the equivalent of spiritual adults to help us learn? Do we need a teacher, a spiritual advisor, a guru? Even a spirit guide? What is the best way for us to learn what we need to grow and progress?

THE GUIDES RESPOND:

All learning and growth starts from a state of not knowing. Everyone has to acquire knowledge and skills to become a builder, nurse, lawyer, computer engineer, parent. No one is born with any type of specialised human knowledge. It all has to be learnt.

However, people certainly do pick up skills and knowledge at different speeds. There are two main reasons for this. The first is they have done something along the same lines in prior lives and so have built up a knowledge base and skill sets appropriate to whatever it is they are learning now. They bring this base level of knowledge and skills to what they are now learning. Those who pick up new learning extraordinarily quickly are likely to have learnt similar things in prior lives. In fact, many choose to develop sets of skills and knowledge bases over consecutive lives to gain mastery in a specific field of human activity. This is a very common multi-life learning strategy.

On the other hand many people find it difficult to learn. This may be because in prior lives they have not in fact done anything like what they are now attempting. So, for them, they are breaking new territory. Another key reason people have learning difficulties is that some kind of psychological blockage is present. For example, in school a certain percentage of children always have a problem with authority and spend their time bucking the system rather than acquiring the knowledge and positive experiences on offer. Others suffer various forms of performance anxiety. Self-doubt, self-deprecation, and feelings of inadequacy are extremely common. All these factors disrupt the learning process.

In this situation actual learning is a secondary issue. What the individual needs to do is to address the blockage. On the other hand, if the individual *is* successful in removing the blockage, he or she will have performed a major life task and will have taken a huge step towards enhancing their openness to learning later in this life, and definitely next time round. Hence prior experience and blockages impact on how quickly or slowly anyone acquires new information and consequently learns and grows.

Another key factor, and we are now specifically addressing the question, is that if you are asking about spiritual guidance, then you are probably not at the child stage. This is because during the early cycles of incarnation individuals focus on connecting with a human body, learning how to interact with it, and acquiring standard human cognitive and social skills. In general, individuals don't start enquiring about what more than the purely physical and social is going on in their lives until they reach the teen phase of their incarnation cycle. There are exceptions, but this is the usual order of things. So it is only after considerable effort has already been made that individuals start wanting to know more.

This means that you who ask these questions are not children. You are at least spiritual teens. And with the teen stage go a number of predictable feelings. One is the joy at discovering new experiences, particularly adult level experiences that you didn't have access to as a child. At the normal teenage level this involves boy-girl, boy-boy and girl-girl interactions. Physiological changes also mean sex comes into view, and with it issues of relationships, desire, frustration, longing, prohibitions, rules, others telling you what to do, loss, grief ... the whole human gamut. Underlying all these experiences is the issue of identity, who you are in relation to others, who you are to yourself, what you want from life, where you fit in.

All this quite natural teen tumult translates directly across to the spiritual teen phase. However, the big difference is that where for the physical teen it is hormones and sexual urges that start bubbling up urgently into their awareness, for the spiritual teen what bubbles up into their awareness are deep urges emanating from the spiritual self. This results in standard teen behaviour. Thus there is an dawning understanding that one is a spirit inside a body relating to others, who are equally a spirit inside a body. The frustrations and longing have to do with being confused and wanting clarity about what is going on. The prohibitions and rules you bump up against are largely religious and social injunctions and dogma, these being barriers that need to be confronted, raged at, jumped over, and inwardly dismantled. You need to learn to interact with those who wish to control your worldview. And underlying it all is a groping towards a new sense of self-identity, one that is constructed by you, for yourself, in the context of what you want to achieve in the domain of human endeavour.

Of course, a fundamental difference between the physical and spiritual teen years is that the teen years last only a few years, from twelve or so to twenty. In contrast, the teen phase of the incarnation cycle usually lasts at least one hundred lives. Spiritually, there is a lot to work through!

There is a another complication with this physical-spiritual comparison. In everyday human life Westerners nominally become adults at twenty-one—although some legal definitions of adulthood come earlier, with individuals able before twenty-one to drive, drink, vote, have sex, cease living with their parents, earn a living, and join the armed forces. In addition, many people still behave like teenagers in their forties, fifties and sixties. So even in ordinary terms being a teenager psychologically has only a glancing relationship with chronological years. This means that in practice there is a blurred demarcation between being a teen and being an adult.

Similarly, on the spiritual level there is a blurring between the teen phase and the adult phase. This is primarily because adulthood covers such a vast swathe of each person's life. A sixty year old has a vast amount more experience than a twenty-one year old. If the sixty year old has learned from life experiences, she or he is mature compared to the twenty-one year old who is usually still quite immature. Spiritually, hundreds of lives are spent developing from immature to mature adult. And at the start of that process there is no overt difference between the savvy teen and the immature adult.

One key point that does differentiate the teen and the adult is that the teen is still being looked after by family or care-givers. Teens are not socially or legally free to do as they wish. Others are looking after them. But once one is an adult one is socially and legally free. The obligation of freedom is that one is expected to sign up to the world, to look after oneself, and to fulfil social obligations such as paying taxes. The plus side is that one is free to pursue one's own interests and to play with other like-minded adults.

This equally applies spiritually. The adult is differentiated from the teen by a willingness to take personal responsibility. Spiritually, this means engaging in activities deliberately chosen so you may have new experiences, enhance current skills, develop new skills, achieve life goals, and help others achieve their goals.

Spiritual adulthood does not necessarily imply engaging in overtly spiritual tasks. This may be the case, but for most individuals it is not. Rather, spiritual adulthood involves taking responsibility for yourself as a spirit living in a body and following through on those plans that you have set yourself to achieve this time round.

Underpinning all this is a growing sense of your own identity. Clarity and certainty about life derives from self-certainty about who you are and what you're about. It can take a long time to obtain this level of certainty! It could be said that the pattern of each life is that it feels like you are always groping towards figuring out what you should be doing. But from a much wider perspective this process is actually part of your progressive evolution. Hesitancy, groping, feeling your way, is fundamental to all learning. And what you learn, the lessons extracted, the knowledge gained, the love involved, all contribute to your evolution as a spiritual identity.

What we have attempted to make clear here is that the fact you are asking these questions means you are likely not in the child phase of your incarnation cycle. You are at least in the teen phase, and very likely in the early or immature adult phase.

So the question becomes: Whether you are a older teen or immature adult, what guidance should you seek? Is it necessary to study with a teacher of some kind, or to seek personal guidance from a disembodied source, such as ourselves. The fact is, you already *are* receiving guidance from the latter source! We acknowledge this is a somewhat facetious statement. But there is certainly much else available, disseminated from other disembodied sources, should you wish to hunt it out.

However, ultimately what is required is focused and sustained inner work. And there is no one-size-fits-all prescription for what is the best guidance to ensure you are effective in your inner work. There is an old saying that students don't need the greatest teacher of all time, they just need a teacher who knows a little more than they do and who is able to impart what they know.

Effective learning requires first a willingness to learn, then a source of knowledge who is able to impart what is required, followed by the student's application of what is imparted. Beyond that we are not willing to go. We are unwilling to state in categorical terms what is best for you. Instead we invite you to examine where you are now in your cycle of learning, the nature of the social environment you find yourself, and the particular advantages and disadvantages that intimately affect your life.

Becoming a spiritual adult begins with taking responsibility for yourself. You have to make your own decisions regarding what is best for you now, at your current stage, in the context of what you seek to achieve and know.

What we *can* give you is absolute assurance that you are being observed and guided. This starts with your own deep self, who is observing and guiding you always. Beyond that are others who care for you personally and with great love, who have your interests entirely at heart.

So don't be timid! It's all before you. Wherever you are in your incarnational cycle is where you are. Take a flying leap! You really are much freer than you could ever conceive!

Just remember, wherever you land, get stuck in. The more you apply yourself, the more will open up to you. And the answers you seek will come flooding in!

Spiritual evolution? Enlightenment? I dunno!

What's this talk of spiritual evolution about? I always thought that at our core we are made of "spiritual stuff," and that all we have to do is learn to contact this stuff inside us and that's it, we become enlightened. That's because the "stuff inside" is part of God, God is perfect, so we become perfect too. Are you saying this isn't how spirituality works? So how is the spiritual process as you see it?

THE GUIDES RESPOND:

All your spiritual enquiries and explorations occur in two directions. The first is into your activities in the world. The second is into the nature of your own awareness.

One direction is external. It involves observing how you behave with others in the world, how you react, what goals you set and achieve, how you deal with frustrations and upsets when pursuing your goals, and how you get yourself back on track to achieve what you set yourself.

The other direction is internal. It involves exploring your own core spiritual nature, of shifting your awareness away from complete engagement with physical and social reality and into what you are within and beyond that. A Buddhist teaching asks, "Show me your face before you were born." This encapsulates what we are referring to.

These two directions are complementary. They may be said to be two sides of the one coin. When you explore your inner nature, you uncover information about why you act the way you do in the world and what your deep relationship is with others. Similarly, when you examine in depth what you are doing in the world, and come to appreciate how and why you relate to others, this tells you much about you at your deep core level.

This is because your deep nature is directly reflected, it directly manifests, in the way you are in the world. So if you examine in an open, detached and unbiased manner how you are in the world, you will discover much of the who, how, what and why of your existence. This includes becoming aware of incidents and choices made in prior lives that are influencing how you behave now and what you are doing this time round.

One direction is not better than the other. Each are equally effective in achieving spiritual level understanding. If you concentrate on looking out at your interactions in the world, then you concentrate on performance and growth. You adopt a developmental outlook and emphasise the need to do and be better. Alternatively, if you concentrate on looking within, which is done by those whose primary practice involves meditation and prayer, then you tend not to talk in terms of development but in terms of enlightenment. So it could be said that an outward focus uses the language of personal growth and development, while those with an inward focus use the language of revelation and transportation, of enlightenment.

In terms of which is preferred, it is just a matter of what you are seeking to achieve this time round. Some individuals focus inwardly because they feel a need to build their sense of their inner spiritual self, while others look outwards because they feel a need to rebalance their self in relation to others. Many do both. Whatever approach is adopted is done out of expediency rather than because one is intrinsically better or more spiritual than the other.

To answer the question about becoming enlightened, yes, there is a state of understanding that may be called enlightenment. But enlightenment is not a one stop shop. That is, there is not a single state you achieve in which you become enlightened and that's it. Rather, as you progressively delve into your own deep self, and as you use your spiritual self to explore non-physical aspects of reality, you undergo experiences that teach you ever more about what is going on. So enlightenment involves a progressive series of states and understandings. To seek enlightenment, then, is to enter a developmental scale, to pass through levels, and to keep growing within. These levels in turn reflect your evolution as a spiritual identity.

The question may be asked, what are these levels of enlightenment? We don't want you to feel like you are being teased, that we are dangling a tasty morsel of information in front of you then withdrawing it. However, we decline in this discussion to name all the levels of enlightenment as they apply in the human domain. We have and will discuss them in depth in other contexts. If you are interested, you may hunt them down.

However, we will state that the first level of enlightenment involves appreciating that you are more than a body, that you are a free-floating spiritual identity. This level requires you not just to know it intellectually, but to have directly experienced your self as more than just your physical body, and to have integrated that understanding into your view of the world. One result will be you no longer fear your body's death. Why? Because you know you cannot die.

The fact is, many people already know this at a deep level within. So this first stage of enlightenment is quite common. In saying this, we wish to indicate that those who have achieved any level of enlightenment are not separated out from others. Enlightenment doesn't make anyone better, or more important, or more spiritual, than anyone else. It just means that that is a task that they have carried out, a box they have ticked in their ongoing developmental process, to use management-speak.

In relation to the phrase "becoming perfect," which is used in the sense that someone who reaches the end of spiritual knowledge becomes perfect, we have two points to make. The first is that there is no end to acquiring knowledge. There is no end to what can be discovered and learned. So there is no final state of perfection. There is only a constant striving to know more and to become more. There is certainly a process of constantly seeking to more perfectly perform what you do. But there is no final state of perfect performance.

The second point is that given a perfecting process occurs within human existence, when discussing what that process leads to we prefer to use the term "mastery." Mastery involves the active application of hard-won skills and knowledge. Anyone can develop mastery in any field of human activity that they choose, provided they make the necessary effort, which usually needs to be sustained over several lifetimes. However, mastery is never perfect, because even those who have mastered a field of endeavour can still make mistakes. Nonetheless, the term "mastery" does acknowledge an extremely high level of accomplishment in the human world.

Whatever goals you speak of, whether they involve inner enlightenment or external mastery, underpinning it all is the evolutionary process by which you progress, life after life, from naive and inexperienced, to knowing and loving, a process in which you become far more than you ever previously were.

If we're all good why is there so much evil?

Mastery and enlightenment? It sounds great. But look at the world: it's a mess. There's starvation, exploitation, oppression, stupidity, lies, violence, wars, torture and murder. Human beings are hardly the poster children for spiritual evolution. How do you line up the horrible human reality with this developmental view? If we're all trying to do the best we can, why is so much of our worst on display? Evil has such a powerful presence in the world, could it be that evil is an actual marauding thing?

THE GUIDES RESPOND:

This is a question that has been asked in many different forms. Historically, this question was asked most frequently in reference to God, with people wanting to know why, if God is good, he has allowed so much evil to exist in the world? The question assumes that God is good and that evil can't come from God, so where does evil come from? The above question is essentially asking the same thing, just in a different form: If people are trying to achieve enlightenment, they surely can't consciously be doing evil, so where does evil come from? Both forms of the question suggest there is a contradiction, in that evil appears to be coming from God, who is good, or from human beings, who are attempting to be good.

In resolving this quandary we will, as the saying goes, kill both birds with one stone. First, reality is not constructed in the way these two forms of the one question assume. God, as the creator of all that is, certainly exists. But what human beings perceive as good and evil do not derive directly or deliberately from God. Good and evil, the two poles of human morality, are a human invention. They cannot be applied to God.

To offer a comparison, the idea of being ignorant or savvy regarding the law cannot be applied to fish. Neither can a piece of ordinary green plastic be proclaimed defective on the grounds it cannot carry out the plant process of photosynthesis. Fish and law, plastic and photosynthesis, don't mix. To put it technically, as philosophers say, these are examples of category errors. You are applying terms relevant in one situation to another situation in which the terms aren't meaningful. Applying the human terms of good and evil to God isn't appropriate. God exists in an entirely different sphere of activity and meaning, far beyond the human.

The situation with respect to human beings striving to evolve into inwardly enlightened and outwardly capable beings, yet doing evil along the way, is more complex. Human beings are certainly able to harm others, sometimes to a depraved extent. There is no denying this. The ways people oppress, coerce, exploit, physically and emotionally damage, maim, torture and kill others is very evident in the world, as the question identifies. To call such activity evil is a perfectly acceptable use of the term.

However, to then extrapolate from this evil behaviour and make a general statement about all reality derived from human behaviour—which people do when they claim that evil exists as some kind of metaphysical or spiritual entity, waiting a moment of weakness so it can enter an individual person and lead them astray—is another example of a category error. It is giving evil a separate identity, independent of human behaviour. This is an error because evil is not an independent entity. The notion of evil is a human invention. It only ever exists as a judgement human beings place on others' behaviour. In this sense, evil is a word human beings use to describe behaviour that harms others. To then extract evil from that destructive behaviour and start calling it a separate thing, functioning in its own right, is an error.

To be very clear about this, we assert "evil" may be used as an adjective to describe person's actions, as in "evil behaviour." But to use "evil" as a noun, and then assert that there is an objectively existing entity that can be named Evil, is a mistake. There is no such thing.

Having cleared that up, the question that is left is, why do people act so destructively towards others? Why do they molest, exploit, harm and murder? Why do they behave evilly?

The simple answer is, some individuals do incarnate with the intention of harming others. But this is actually much rarer than you think. We'll come back to this shortly. In practice, the two most common reasons for the occurrence of what human beings call "evil behaviour" may be identified as collateral damage and self-defence. We'll explain.

As we have stated in earlier responses, everyone incarnates with a life plan. For some, this plan involves carrying out certain tasks, getting particular things done. During their life some then go at their self-chosen tasks with single-minded, even myopic, devotion. And they end up steam-rolling other people. It's not nice. But it's what happens. This is collateral damage. It happens on both large and small scales. On the small scale it occurs when, say, a boss has to follow through on a business decision and the lives of workers are seriously upset, even turned upside down. It happens on a grand scale when politicians make a policy call and thousands or millions have their lives destroyed, whether by crashes in the market place, famine or war.

In saying this, we note that the specific acts are not necessarily what was planned, prior to incarnation, by the individual who enacts them. But being the particular person who can perform such an act, with the psychological traits necessary to get into a position to initiate that act and carry it out, is certainly selected prior to incarnation.

The second reason, self-defence, occurs when people defend themselves and the effect of their decision is greater than they expect. This occurs when an individual decides to follow a certain line of action, other people call them out on it, and they then have to push back harder in order to defend their original position or decision. This has occurred recently in terms of terror legislation around the world. The security and intelligence gathering communities decided they needed greater access to communications data. The politicians knew there would be push-back from savvy and vocal members of the public, so they attempted to keep everything secret. The leaders in the security and intelligence community saw a vacuum in the decision-making and so pushed what they were doing to the limit. Then, when the savvy and vocal found out what was happening and made open what was sought to be kept secret, the politicians hardened their position with new legislation. The result is a situation where what began as a simple desire to protect countries has blown up into a situation in which everyone is spied on.

We make no claim as to whether this is a good or bad situation. It is, from our perspective, just what it is. However, it indicates two things. One is that self-defensiveness can escalate a situation very quickly, leading to much greater impact than originally intended. The other is that the very notions of good and evil are shown to be human social constructs. For some people gathering the data of everyone on the planet is good, while for others the very same behaviour is bad. Which position you adopt depends on your social perspective.

The same could be said of terrorism itself. At one time Nelson Mandela's African National Congress was considered a terrorist organisation. Mandela, as symbolic head of that organisation, subsequently became leader of South Africa and was then widely lauded as a good man. We reiterate, whether anything is good or evil depends entirely on your perspective. And all perspectives are human social constructs.

Accordingly, harmful and destructive behaviour most commonly results, first, when people have a task to complete and in their single-minded pursuit they hurt others along the way, and, second, when people defend themselves and their response escalates the original behaviour into something harmful to others. Almost all so-called evil actions occur as a result of these two behaviours. They are not behaviours deliberately performed to hurt others. Hurt is a by-product.

As regards people wilfully and deliberately harming others, which is the traditional view of what an evil individual does, this behaviour can fall into a number of categories.

Collateral damage can escalate when people initially generate harm with a decision or action, subsequently become aware that others are being hurt, but their single-mindedness pushes them to stay the course and carry on, no matter what. To protect themselves from the fall-out they frequently harden themselves by deliberately fostering indifference. Both economic policies and acts of war that generate extensive collateral damage are maintained by groups and individuals who use indifference to shut themselves off from data regarding the numbers of hurt, maimed and dead. Deliberately adopted indifference also keeps them from honestly reviewing the impact they are having on others.

A second behaviour often used to sustain this kind of myopic destructive approach is willed self-defensiveness. Willed self-defensiveness can escalate into a situation in which one person deliberately hurts another to keep defending themselves. For example, a whistleblower may highlight errors, lies or self-interested actions performed by another. The individual (or individuals) identified as doing wrong may then decide to take out the whistleblower, whether by reputation or physically. They may subsequently shut down anyone else who follows up on the whistleblower's claims or demise. Those in power have often made this type of escalating willed self-defensive choice.

Another type of escalation occurs when someone carries out an act they know they shouldn't, then reactively does all they can to prevent others from finding out. Sometimes they may really be directly threatened with exposure. At others they are just attempting to lower the odds of being exposed. Or they may even misinterpret what someone is doing and erroneously take out someone who wasn't a threat at all. Whichever they use, they are again defending themselves, this time in a way that others don't perceive.

Yet another example of escalation occurs when individuals lash out violently, maiming or even killing another, then feel they have nothing to lose and keep going. Violence then becomes habitual behaviour for such a person. This type of individual most commonly survives among career criminals, to whom violence is a form of communication. Sometimes uninvolved bystanders are accidentally caught up in the violence. Many people would view a criminal killing another criminal as a social good, whereas a criminal killing a bystander is evil. Incidentally, habitual violence also commonly becomes a behavioural default among police and those in the armed forces.

It is not that these people incarnate with the express aim of maiming and killing others. It is more that they enter a social environment in which violence is condoned, and they not only take such behaviour on board, but they go overboard with it, going further than others in the same situation do.

Are serial killers born with an intent to murder, perhaps torture others? Yes. Is this because they have an evil soul? No. We reiterate, they are *being* evil. They are not an innately evil being. The individual serial killer is inwardly tortured, psychologically twisted even, and is having to work their way through behaviours that have been inflicted on them by others in prior lives. What do we mean by this?

It is well known that domestic violence is generational. So if a child is beaten or sexually molested by a parent, he or she is more likely to repeat the same behaviour than someone who was never beaten or molested as a child. Behaviours become imprinted from one generation to the next. This also occurs from one life to the next.

Many people are in pain at deep levels within. All have to deal with it in the best way they can. Sometimes the way to exorcise pain is to enact it, just as the best way to heal a boil is to let the pus out. If others are exposed to the pus they may become ill themselves. If others are violently exposed to evil behaviour and deeply imprinted by it, they may subsequently act evilly.

This equally applies to those who deliberately, even with great pleasure, torture others. It makes no difference whether torture is done in the name of religious belief, to protect the secrets or safety of a state, to ensure a continued flow of profits, or is entirely personally motivated. Anyone who is capable of mutilating and inflicting horrendous pain on another is clearly inwardly unbalanced. It is an imbalance that will be addressed in future incarnations. But, in the meantime, great psychological scars are created for both victim and perpetrator. These scars not only require considerable effort to be healed, but all lumpy psychological traits have to be smoothed out. Smoothing out involves the perpetrator physically and emotionally correcting what they have done, forgiveness being granted by the victim, reconciliation between perpetrator and victim occurring, and for all aberrant and reactive behaviours in both to be utterly abraded away.

So it is not that evil is out there stalking anyone. It is rather that humans engage in harmful behaviour, behaviour that is labelled evil, and that behaviour impacts on other individuals and generates more behaviour of the same.

Is this an endless cycle? No. As just indicated in relation to dealing with the aftermath of torture, all individuals who behave destructively, progressively, over lives, absorb their life lessons and overcome their tendency to behave in ways that harm others. This inner growth naturally occurs as individuals grow from child, through teen, to inexperienced adult, to experienced adult. It is all part of the growing pains of learning to be a spirit occupying a human body and living with others in the complex human world.

Life seems so laborious. Isn't there a shortcut?

So human beings are responsible for the mess we've made of the world. And I guess when we've all lived a few more lives we'll be more adult and mature and life for everyone will improve. But I can't see that happening in the near future. Is there a way to short circuit the whole learning process, with its built-in mistakes, and reduce the pain and misery faster?

THE GUIDES RESPOND:

The human world can often be a tough place to dwell in. It can also be repetitive, tedious, boring. There are many disappointments. Just surviving day to day for most involves worry regarding what will happen in the future, and concerns about children and loved ones today. So when you hear advice such as ours that living is about learning life lessons, and that once you have learnt those lessons you become a better, more evolved individual, it is understandable that you naturally wonder if there is a way to speed up the whole process.

We have bad news in this respect. No, you cannot speed up the process. At least, not in the way that is being asked.

Certainly, some individuals have gone through their reincarnational cycle in fewer lives than the average. We are thinking in particular of the well known example of the individual who was known in his last life as the Buddha (the use of "he" is nominal because, of course, spirits have no gender). Many other unknown individuals have spent fewer or considerably more lives than the norm of one thousand as they go through their cycle of incarnations in order to reach that evolved state in which incarnation is no longer continued.

Is anything to be gained experiencing a cycle that is longer or shorter than the norm? No. Just as different plants in the garden have differing life cycles, some lasting a season and others many seasons, so some identities take more lives and others fewer lives to develop skills and learn the lessons that human incarnation offers. As we have stated elsewhere, there is no reward or stigma attached to either outcome. It just is what it is. Just as the plants in the garden are what they are. And the conditions of human life—stimulating, tedious, challenging, boring, repetitive, or fresh every day—are what they are.

Of more concern to us—to reflect this common human terminology back to you—is that people often don't make the most of the opportunities that are in front of them. For example, people say they are bored by their job, or by their career, or by a relationship. But if they brought more of themselves to what they are doing, if they set themselves new tasks to perform, overlaid and in addition to what they already do each day, then that repeated activity would have an entirely new layer of challenge added to it.

All jobs have cycles of repetition built into them. This is inevitable. Whether it takes five minutes, five years, or even five decades, eventually that repetition wears people down. But if you set yourself a new task within that job, such as working on your people skills, or learning not to react the way you always do in a certain situation, or learning to put yourself in others' shoes, or if you strive to guide people to preferred results by steering them from behind rather than directing them from the front (or visa versa), then the familiar daily routine becomes enriched, more challenging, more meaningful. The challenge you lay over familiar tasks effectively makes them into new activities. You also, in the process, stimulate your own deep level growth. Which is what the whole incarnation process is about.

From our perspective, this issue of people not making the most of life opportunities is very significant. We know that during our cycles of incarnations we certainly avoided dealing with difficulties, ran away from responsibilities, and tried to put off grappling with the less pleasant aspects of being a spirit in a human body. We also complained of boredom, tedium, repetition. As we observed, this is part of being human. But it is also an attitude that impeded our growth. And it equally contributes to your evolution being slower than desired.

If you want to work your way through your cycle of incarnations faster, what you need to do is what is most difficult: face up to all the issues that trouble you in your life. This is because everyone likes to engage in what they enjoy. But few are as enthusiastic in addressing the unpleasant aspects of their psychological make up. The unpleasant includes all the unresolved negative feelings that swill around inside you, the anger you wallow in when it flares up then put "out of sight and out of mind" after it dies away, all your regrets, your unhappinesses, your pains, your feelings of rejection, of being slighted, your despair. Face up to everything you can bear to. For these are what are holding you back. They're not holding you back because they are "bads" that are tainting your inner "good." They are holding you back because they consist of unresolved psychological traits that are in play in your life. When you resolve them you will be able to experience moment to moment living with more happiness and joy, and as a result you will be much less inclined to want to get through your cycles of incarnation so quickly. You'll also be free to move on to, as is said, bigger, brighter and more exciting things.

Such psychological issues arise because no one gets right the task of being human immediately and fully. Being human involves multiple skills that you necessarily take multiple lives to acquire. To speak by analogy, becoming a high wire walker takes repeated efforts. As a trainee you start on a low wire, just above the ground. You fall off and get back up, all the while training your body to balance and your mind not to interfere, and especially not to fear. Gradually, you become more confident, more skillful, and you raise the wire higher and higher. The same occurs with human incarnation. At first you take baby steps, setting low level and attainable goals. Then, as you acquire skills and develop confidence in your abilities, you take on more complex situations and tasks. You succeed in some areas, fail in others. But you keep trying. And gradually, over hundreds of lives, you rise higher and higher on the high wire of human existence.

This brings us to another important issue. No one else ever tells you how high or low you must go. You set the height of the wire. You decide what you want to take on next, what you want try your hand at, what you don't want to engage with. You also decide on what percentage success you are likely to have, by which we mean how easy or difficult the circumstances of your next incarnation will be. We'll explain.

When you select a new incarnation, you choose the overall learning goals. You also choose the tasks which will help you achieve those goals. And you set the degree of difficulty. Some spiritual identities like to play it safe and so choose a small goal that will take them one incremental step forwards their overall evolution. Others adopt a riskier approach, taking on multiple tasks. This complexity means they are also more likely to fail than identities who select less demanding tasks. Risk-takers often fall off the high wire in spectacular fashion. But they learn a great deal in the process. They then climb into their next body and repeat their selected tasks, succeeding at some, failing at others, until they get their performance right. They then move on to another set of equally ambitious tasks. Or, alternatively, they may decide to have a "breather" life, or series of lives, so they can process what they have experienced. Whether identities choose to take small steps or large steps is of significance only to the identity concerned. It all just reflects the different ways that identities go about experiencing and learning.

What we are attempting to indicate here is that what you get out of your life is reflected in what you put in. In this life the greater depth and intensity with which you consider your life, and the more you try to achieve, the more enriched your life will be. But this is your choice. You may cruise in this life if that is what you want. You may dig a little into what is going on within you. Or you may dig to a great depth.

The same applies across lives. Spiritual identities approach the opportunity of incarnation with different goals, differing intensities, and engage at different depths. Everyone has lives when they take a shallow trajectory and other lives when they dive deep, and yet other lives when they feel behind the eight ball and are trying to catch up inside themselves with what they have experienced.

The point is, there is no right or wrong way to approach incarnation. Identities start with one concept in mind when they begin their incarnation cycle, such as wanting to be like the evolved identities they initially met in the spiritual domain, but once they discover what is possible they usually radically alter their goals, and themselves in the process. This is possible over the course of hundreds of lives. Others remain very consistent and recognisable throughout their entire reincarnation cycle.

This same growth outcome is seen among human beings, when you meet friends you went to school with decades later. Some are just like they used to be, displaying the same fundamental characteristics. Others are changed, perhaps almost unrecognisably. And we attach no approval or approbation to either outcome. It is what it is.

To conclude, if you wish to "reduce the pain and misery faster," or, to speak more positively, if you wish to more rapidly develop your skills to a higher level, then address what is holding you back. Because the less that is dragging you back into the familiar, the repetitive and the mundane, the higher and faster you will fly.

We acknowledge our advice seems rather mundane and sensible. But that is because it is actually the best and fastest way to progress.

Does God fire thunderbolts at us when we screw up?

What about God? We're told God is always watching and occasionally flings a thunderbolt from His hand when we do something wrong. (I guess it has to be His left hand because Jesus is sitting on His right hand—the Bible says so). So how does the system work? When we mess up how is retribution organised? And who is really in charge? We're told God is, that He controls everything. But who is God? And why is He doing this to me? What's His angle? I say 'He' because that's how we're taught to talk, but does God even have a gender?

THE GUIDES RESPOND:

From our perspective, having an overview of human existence, the idea of human beings trying to dodge thunderbolts flung by God is highly humorous. That we ourselves fervently believed such things during our own repeated sojourns on Earth makes this situation no less amusing.

Human beings love to ascribe all kinds of phenomena to God. Whether it is their ability to do well in life, or obstacles that stop them achieving their plans, or whenever something bad happens to them, or even when they find that elusive car park that presents itself just when they need it, the notion that God is responsible for each and every positive and negative life event is widely believed. It is, of course, a completely erroneous belief.

We referred previously to the notion of God as creator. Everything that exists in the extensive continuum from the spiritual to the physical has been created. This includes us, you and every kind of spiritual identity. If you wish, you can call the creator God. We have done so here only because that is a familiar conventional term.

However, it is also the case that the word "God" comes with significant historical baggage, most of it wrong. Is God as creator a variety of superhuman being? No. Does God as creator have a body? No. Does God have a sex? No. Does God throw thunderbolts, or utilise any other kind of retributive mechanism, for dealing with people when they mess up? No.

The truth is, God as creator of everything is so far beyond not just your human experience, but your human ability to conceive or know, that to use God to explain what you find pleasing or displeasing in your life is inappropriate. Indeed, it is completely inadequate. And this is due, as we discussed earlier, to a category error. God as creator cannot be yoked to human notions of what you find pleasing or displeasing in your life.

We do not use the words "pleasing" and "displeasing" facetiously. We observe that these two words denote a principal category human beings use to define the values of good and bad, propitious and evil. A life event that is pleasing people call a social, economic, philosophic, religious or spiritual good. And events that are displeasing are called bad or evil. Furthermore, as we also discussed earlier, what people find pleasing or displeasing depends entirely on the agenda they have personally adopted in relation to their own lives.

You asked what God's system or angle is in relation to human existence. We pose the question back to you: What agenda, system or angle have you adopted in relation to your own life? Whenever life events occur that please or displease you, instead of seeing these events as being the universe's God rewarding you for doing well or punished you for for messing up, rather ask: What have I done that has led to my life circumstances now giving me positive or negative feedback? Look first for causes in your own choices, avoidances, behaviour and psychological traits. Because whatever agenda you are enacting, whatever system or strategy you have put in place to cope with life, whatever angle you're exploiting, that is where the cause of what pleases or displeases you will be found.

To put this very simply: Leave God out of it. Instead put yourself at the centre of your quest to understand. If you adopt this outlook, the question shifts from wondering what God is doing to you and is replaced by the question of what you are doing to yourself.

It is easy to be critical of life. It is more difficult to be critical of yourself. In asserting this, we are not suggesting you engage in some kind of blame game. Or in a bitch session in which you are the target of your own name calling. This is counter-productive. As are all forms of bitching, blaming and name-calling.

We raise this because historically people have repeatedly blamed God for the calamities that struck them down. They have scorned God for not helping them when they called. They have cursed God for not hearing them and for abandoning them. They have even called into question God's very existence and purpose.

This blaming behaviour is always projection. It is an attempt people make to divert the focus from themselves. When calamities fall the most productive approach is to examine your own choices and try to discern what you could have done differently to achieve a better outcome—however "better" is defined in the particular context. When the aid that is sought doesn't arrive, or when people don't go to others' aid when asked, they need to question themselves and identify what they did and didn't do. They would be better off castigating themselves, not God or life or fate or other people, when they feel abandoned, because what is actually happening is that they don't hear their own deep self calling. The existence and purpose they should ponder isn't God's, it's their own.

Over the millennia God has taken the brunt of humanity's inability to live soundly in the world. In this sense, the notion of God as conveyer of thunderbolts who punishes people when they do wrong is a way for individuals to avoid addressing their own inadequacies. They feel something along the lines of: I've done bad, so punish me God! That way they pass the consequences for their messing up onto someone else who is then left to deal with it. They equate punishment with making up for errors of judgement and performance. This is childish behaviour.

Adults face up to their errors and attempt to correct them. If they are brave they can attempt to do so this time round, in this life. And, to be frank, sooner is usually better than later. But later will do, in another life, if that is how circumstances play out, for example, if the person or people for whom you need to correct your error are not around any more, having moved away or died.

So we now return to our central theme: Do not project what pleases or displeases you onto anyone or anything else, whether that be an individual, chance, fate, or God. Do not say that what pleases or displeases you is God's reward or punishment for being good or bad. And do not displace your need to make up for your own errors onto anyone else, human or extra-human, waiting for them to punish you so you don't have to take any purposeful correcting action yourself.

Instead, to adapt a popular term, adult up! An adult dispels childish illusions. An adult takes responsibility for prior actions. Adults do the best they can in whatever circumstances they find themselves, circumstances that their choices, behaviour and agenda have largely brought them into.

Generate your own thunderbolts that blast to pieces the illusions you have constructed about the world and yourself. And no ducking! Stand up bravely to the blast. In the aftermath you'll discover the experience isn't as harrowing as you feared. In fact, you'll appreciate it not just as beneficial, but as greatly pleasing to your deep self!

Is there a God team?
Who's batting on my side?

Okay, so God is a distant unknowable creator. But is there just one God? Some people talk about a spiritual hierarchy. Does God have a team? Is there one God for the Earth, another God for our solar system, another for our universe? Does this God team chat on a spiritual internet and make divine skype calls to the gods of other universes? If so, who is their God? And is one of them looking after me? If I learn enough over a zillion lifetimes, will I be like God? And will it be worth it?

THE GUIDES RESPOND:

Underlying this question is an anxiety. Are human beings in general, and you in particular, being looked after by those in the spiritual realm? The answer to this is an unequivocal yes. No one is abandoned. Ever. No matter how it appears. Everyone has attention continuously directed onto them. Help always comes when it is needed.

On the other hand, this doesn't mean you are directly guided every moment of your existence. Quite the contrary. You are free to explore, exploit, enjoy and mess up as you choose. No one in the spiritual domain will step in and stop you doing so. You are quite free within the limits of choice you set for yourself before you were born.

Of course, people often feel they have been abandoned. As we commented in the previous response, human beings, or to be more exact, spiritual identities living within a human body and psyche, often feel that they have been abandoned by God, angels, or saints, or whatever other spiritual identity they have been conditioned to expect or have forged for themselves. In fact, issues around feeling abandoned or lost or purposeless derive from a lack of perspective.

Those in the spiritual domain who observe and care for those "below" (we use this word as a metaphor—and it is only a metaphor, not a reflection of the actual relationship between the so-called physical and spiritual domains) can see much further due to having a wider perspective than the embodied. Those "above" can see that the struggling individual is like a child in a playground. The child thinks it is lost and starts crying, calling out for help. (A child usually calls for its mother or father, while adults often cry out to a religious figure.) But what the crying child doesn't know is that a short distance away, just round the corner of the path, is the solution to their problem. And when they turn the corner their immediate trouble will be solved.

When that occurs, the troubled individual often makes the claim to others that they were helped by whoever they conceive does so, whether that be a guardian angel, saint, or God. This is erroneous thinking. What most typically happens in such a situation is that those "above" see that the problem will be resolved quite soon. So they do nothing. That is their help. It is help because their inaction allows troubled individuals to find the solution themselves. And this enables them to stand, like an adult, on their own two feet.

Of course, if someone is in a very bad way inside themselves, or if they are getting ever more confused, or if a key turning point in their life is approaching and they are too unclear to make the decision that accords with their life plan, direct intervention will almost always come. Whether or not the individual pays attention to that intervention and is guided by it is, of course, another question. What form does intervention take? Several forms are possible.

Most common is a cue. Cues come from a variety of directions, and usually at times when the individual is considering a key life decision. A cue may be emotional, mental or physical in form. The purpose is to help ensure an individual acts in accordance with the pre-selected life plan.

A cue may come as a feeling a person has that they should do something in particular, or go somewhere, or attend a meeting, or explore a specific opportunity. Individuals may be in a book shop and feel directed to pick up a certain book. Or they may pick up the book without being aware they have been "nudged" to do so. Alternatively, they may have a dream, be talking to someone, or a thought may pop into their head, each of which provides information that lingers in their attention and indicates a particular direction to go or a decision that could be made.

Cues may particularly fruitfully arrive during prayer or meditation. Cues are often ignored because individuals are easily distracted by other competing feelings and ideas, resulting in the cue arriving and vanishing without making much impression. Prayer and meditation provide better circumstances for a cue to make an impression because the individual has less going on mentally and emotionally and much less physical distraction. The result is a stronger, clearer line of communication between the individual's everyday mind and the deeper self. In such situations, and especially if the individual is specifically praying or meditating in search of guidance regarding what to do, that individual is much more open to what arrives.

Stronger interventions occur when those "above" directly and physically intervene in an individual's life. This may involve stopping them getting on board an aircraft, having them arriving early or late at an event, or even causing a bullet to misfire in a gun. This can and does happen. But not on a regular basis. The reason intervention of this kind occurs is because the opportunities provided by the life plan have not been fulfilled. In this sense intervention is done to keep a life on course and to facilitate meetings and opportunities that were planned prior to birth, which a premature death would stop from occurring.

Not all lives have such interventions. Chance is generally allowed to run its course. But everyone, from time to time throughout their overall cycle of incarnations, has a direct intervention in their life of this kind. To a degree it is only common sense that such interventions are made, particularly when a number of lives are linked and if one or two key people died prematurely that would impact not just on their life plans, but on the life plans of all those others linked to them.

So do miracles occur? Yes. Do they occur frequently? No. Are those people special in some way whose lives experience a "miraculous" intervention? No. It is a pragmatic decision made by those in a position to do so to help facilitate a life's fullest realisation.

Who do the intervening? Is there a "God team" orchestrating miracles across the multiverses? We enjoy the question. But, as usual, the answer is more humdrum than this exotic notion proposes.

In everyday human existence the people who care most about you, the ones who most often come to your aid when you need it, are family and friends who care for you. The same applies on the spiritual level. So the question becomes, who are these caring spiritual family and friends?

Every human being is a member of a soul group. Soul groups typically number between 800 and 1200. This means you are one of a group of incarnating identities numbering somewhere within this range. This group is your immediate spiritual family. Again, as a general statement, around one third of these individual fragments are incarnated at any one time. Those who are between lives have their own tasks to carry out. Nonetheless, some among them are always connected to and "keeping an eye out" on those in their soul group family who are occupying bodies. So this is one level of spiritual care.

A second level consists of those members of similar soul groups. To offer a general indication only, most incarnated individuals interact with an extended family group which includes another six soul groups. Members of these other groups may be likened to cousins. But, as with human cousins, you may form stronger bonds with some of them than with your own close siblings. This extended family consists of somewhere between 56,000 and 84,000 individual spiritual identities. So no matter how you feel, you are never abandoned and alone!

Throughout your cycle of approximately one thousand lives you will interact with, and become friends, colleagues, lovers, enemies, mentors, parents and children of a greater or smaller number of these close and extended family members. How many depends on you. Just as human beings are gregarious, or the life of the party, or enjoy staying behind the scenes, or don't go out much at all, so spiritual identities vary in degrees of outwardness and inwardness.

Of course, you will also live lives, perhaps a number of lives, with other identities outside this extended family group. But as regards ongoing assistance, most help comes from those who care most about you, that being members of your close and extended family.

A third level of assistance comes from those more experienced spiritual identities who oversee and guide individual identities such as you through their series of incarnations. Some among these remain aware of what you are going through and have the expertise, when required, to provide cues or to directly intervene.

Yet another level of observation is provided by those who, like us, have completed their own cycle of incarnations and now exist as a reintegrated spiritual entity in which all members are rejoined. We have a wider view again compared to those we have indicated, a view that comes from having completed what you are going through. We have our own tasks of guidance, such as is manifesting now in this communication. A key issue is that spiritual perspectives and forms of guidance need to be periodically updated to reflect cultural changes. That updating task is one of our current functions. We also provide direct instruction to those who foster communication with us.

Beyond us are wider perspectives again that reflect greater levels of experience. We communicate with these identities as we learn how to best perform our self-selected tasks. This level is not God. At this stage we decline to say any more about them.

Finally, there is the guidance that emanates from your own spiritual self. You have great experience and knowledge within you. You, at the level of your spiritual identity, selected a life plan and life tasks. It is in your own interest to ensure you perform them. So your own spiritual self is constantly making suggestions, initiating cues, giving you dreams, recommending a book to read, indicating a gathering worth attending, pointing out a person worth meeting, or drawing your attention to choice phrases that are useful. Your own spiritual self wants your life to be successful on all levels. So it drops hints and intervenes whenever it is able—sometimes successfully, often unsuccessfully, given that you, at your everyday level, have many other inputs and distractions to deal with day by day, hour by hour, minute by minute.

This indicates something of the range of help that is available to you, the number of those who care about you and are actively "keeping an eye out" and are aware of you and what you are doing.

Do those in the spiritual domain who care for you make skype-like calls across the multiverse? Simply, no. There are actually many kinds of spiritual beings occupied with unimaginable quantities and varieties of tasks. Some are goal-oriented. Some just play. Others are marauders. Others gregariously go out to engage others. Others keep to themselves. The vast majority have not the slightest knowledge of, or interest in, what is happening on Earth. So in this sense the only spiritual beings who would "skype" about humanity and what is happening on Earth are those who are already most intimately involved in what is happening on Earth. This means the multiverse falls out of the communication equation.

As regards those who are focused on Earth—and there are more than you could imagine!—there is no central command in which a yearly plan is drawn up, roles are given out, tasks are listed, tasks are performed, and reporting back occurs. Nonetheless, plans are certainly in place. However, these plans are like your life plan.

Before you incarnated, possibilities were identified, you made selections from those possibilities, and you put plans into place to actualise your selected possibilities. But your plans come together, or are stretched, or break completely, according to what you and other involved people actually choose to do in the midst of life. In the same way, we also establish plans, then work with them or adjust them according to how the plans play out in actuality. Other spiritual level beings do the same.

So there is no big pre-destined plan. What there is, is a constant intent to help the embodied grow and evolve. This is one fundamental difference between those embodied in human existence and the spiritually disembodied. The embodied have mixed intentions. Some are helpful, others are looking after themselves, yet others feel guilty and seek expiation, and others again have a God-complex and want to punish those who they feel are unworthy. Many people have multiple intentions, working at cross purposes. In contrast, those in the spiritual realm all consistently possess the same intent: to help you become all you may become.

At the end of the process will you become like God and will it be worth it? Who knows. We will inform you when we get there! In the meantime we are all on a marvellous adventure. We were once where you are. In some future moment you will be where we are now. You will help others as we are doing. And you will prepare to follow us into the beyond to discover whatever comes next. Is it worth it? We can only speak from our own perspective. It is! It is!

How does a gut feeling differ from true insight?

How can we know that a gut feeling is something to be listened to, that it comes from our higher self, and isn't just pre-programming, echoes of a past experience, or reflects our reluctance to deal with something? How do I distinguish between something happening for a spiritual or karmic reason and it only happening through choice or accident, or just from being human? Related to all this, what's the difference between emotion and intuition?

THE GUIDES RESPOND:

This is a key question that must be faced by anyone who wishes to make sustained contact with their deep self. No matter how experienced you are, no matter how many years you have participated in the "spirituality game", being able to discern where information is coming from inside you remains a crucial skill.

However, before discussing this we need to address an issue of terminology. Instead of the phrase "gut feeling" we prefer the term "inner cue." This is because all kinds of impulses emanate from different parts of your psyche. Your stomach, your hormones, your emotions, your genitals, and your socially conditioned self all continuously send impulses to your everyday mind suggesting, sometimes demanding, that you do one action rather than another, say these or those words, or make this choice over that.

All these impulses may be termed "gut feelings" in the sense they emanate from these various physical and social parts of your psyche. What these parts have in common is that they are transitory. Each is embedded in your sub-identity, which is made up of all the physical, social, emotional and intellectual aspects of your current identity. The "gut feelings" that arise as impulses from these various aspects of you are transitory in the sense that they come and go in reaction to changing life circumstances. They will also vanish completely when your body dies and your current sub-identity expires with it.

In contrast, inner cues emanate from your spiritual self. The spiritual self will continue to exist after your current sub-identity dies. In this sense, inner cues are neither transitory nor do they come and go. Instead, they remain constant and consistent impulses within you. Why aren't you aware of them? Because all those other voices within you, all those various gut feelings, attract so much of your attention and occupy so much of your time. Inner cues are very different in nature.

We have stated that inner cues emanate from your spiritual self. What is the purpose of inner cues? Their purpose is simply to keep you on track with fulfilling your life plan. Inner cues are that straight forward. They are sent by your spiritual self into your everyday awareness to keep returning your attention to what you are here to achieve this time round.

At times inner cues may become very insistent. This often occurs when a key turning point in your life approaches. Key turning points are times when you need to make a decision, or go on a journey, or attend a meeting, or interact with a particular person in a particular time and place, in order to progress your life plan.

Inner cues take various forms. They may arrive in the form of dreams, as repeated thoughts, as emotional feelings such as frustration or a desire to go somewhere, or in the form of a deep urge that says "this is the right thing to do." Basically, any repeated inner urge to do or choose what you ordinarily wouldn't needs to be closely examined because it is likely to be an inner cue emanating from the spiritual self.

What interrupts the arrival of inner cues, and what prevents their adoption once they do arrive, is resistance. Resistance also takes many forms. But behind all these forms is fear. Fear almost always arises from prior negative experiences, whether undergone in this life or during previous lives.

So we can say there are two main reasons inner cues are not heard and acted on. The first is that there are variety of impulses surging around inside you that, in effect, generate a cacophony of voices shouting within, competing for your attention, and so you don't hear the very subtle voice of your spiritual self. That voice is drowned out. The second reason is that there are aspects of your own psyche that resist the message when you do hear it.

Having clarified our terms we can now return to the question, which asks (at least, in our restructured version): How does one differentiate between inner cues and gut feelings?

The first task is to quieten down the inner cacophony. Basically, you need to establish a clearing among all the urges that surge through your body and shout in your mind. You then need to learn to settle into that quiet clearing and open up your attentive mind to subtle kinds of input. In such a quiet state you will not only be able to clearly differentiate between inner cues and gut feelings, but you will also be able to establish a dialogue between your everyday mind and your spiritual self. This dialogue should be seen as a goal to be achieved by all those who seek to explore their spiritual nature.

So how do you achieve this helpful inner state? Practising meditation, prayer and repeating mantras gives you practice at holding back rowdy thoughts, quietening your mind, and focusing your attention. In some circles reference is made to the "monkey mind" that grabs at whatever thought or feeling happens to be passing through your awareness. This is a useful analogy.

It is a condition of human existence that thoughts, feelings, sensations and urges constantly wash through you. These cannot be stopped completely. The only person who does not experience hunger, thirst, a desire for shelter, or a need for companionship and care, is a dead person. So these phenomena are a completely natural, completely expected condition of human existence. The key to dealing with them is not to suppress them but rather to be able to stop the "monkey mind" reaching out and grabbing them. Learning to do so is a necessary preliminary.

Next you need to open up your awareness to your spiritual self. This is a difficult inner move for many people, as this is where resistance enters the picture. Fear of the unknown provides a fundamental resistance. What you have to understand in relation to this fear is that it is your sub-identity in this life that is fearing, not your spiritual self, not you in your deep self.

"You" in your current human identity are a genetically defined, socially programmed human being who has undergone certain experiences since birth that have shaped how "you" react to whatever life throws your way. "You" have buried fears that first arose during childhood. And "you" possess reflexive psychological defensive and coping mechanisms that have formed to help "you" rebalance when fears arise and enable "you" to remain relatively stable in your social relations. "You" additionally have even more deeply buried negative experiences from previous lives, some of which, not all, also bubble under deep beneath your everyday awareness.

So there are multiple sources for resistance to making a bridge between your everyday awareness and your spiritual self.

By "bridge" what we refer to is an ability to sustain contact with your deeper spiritual self and seek its input whenever you wish. As we have just pointed out, this is the goal. On the other hand, it is quite possible for anyone to receive input, whether that input consists of an inner cue from their spiritual self related to achieving the life plan or just some sensible advice on how to deal with a problem of the day. This can and does occur regularly. The problem, as the question identifies, is how can you know whether or not input present in your awareness comes from your spiritual self?

The best way to know for sure is to work on all the psychological factors that generate resistance within you. This means identifying, facing up to, grappling with, and eliminating, all those psychological traits that plague you within. Such work begins by dealing with psychological coping mechanisms that everyone uses to deal with hassles in their adult lives, mechanisms that actually have their source in childhood upbringing. Everyone's major fears go back to this period in their life. Basically, you need to smooth out all the bumps and swirls and jagged edges that play through your socialised self.

An analogy for what is required is being in a carpenter's workshop and being given a chair that has had a very tough life. Let's say it has an arm broken, its legs are wobbly, chunks are gouged out of its back, and its padding is non-existent. Much work is required to tidy up the chair and make it functional again. You need to do the same to your conditioned and programmed socialised self. You need to make it stable, serviceable, and no longer wobbled by fear or any other negative emotional reaction. Achieving this will help ensure you are in a situation within yourself to make consistent and coherent contact with your deep spiritual self, that your psychological makeup is a stable and fully functioning "chair" in which your spiritual self can sit. This will ensure you are in good shape to make sense of inner cues when they arrive.

To recapitulate. We identify two crucial aspects in regard to inner cues. First you need to clear a space within and work to make yourself quiet enough to recognise when a cue has arrived. This assumes you have achieved some control over your monkey mind and dealt at least to a preliminary degree with negative emotions and psychological resistances. Second, you need to confirm the cue's validity. That is, at the level of your everyday mind, you need to be sure that the cue is in fact a cue and not some suggestive, seductive, or horrifying impulse emanating from another part of your psyche.

Confirming a cue's validity can be confusing. The fact is, people can and do spend years spinning around inside themselves trying to figure out whether or not to follow a cue, and all the while that cue genuinely emanates from their spiritual self. The problem, in a nutshell, comes down to trust. How can they trust themselves that they are following the right impulse and so are about to do the right thing? This inability to trust their own cues leads to a state of uncertainty. Then all kinds of negative emotions follow, such as anxiety, depression, feelings of being lost, of being abandoned, feelings of rejection and hurt. Being able to validate inner cues and so definitely know that they *are* cues, or that they are rather gut feelings, cuts through all this inner turmoil.

How then does one validate inner cues? What is required is to set up a process for confirming where impulses come from. People can establish all kinds of tests to confirm cues. Many try to test God, asking for a sign of some kind. Others of a more secular nature seek signs in nature, such as seeing a particular form, colour or even situation. These methods are not recommended. The best and most efficient way to confirm that an inner cue is valid is by asking your spiritual self. Of course, this is much more easily said than done.

Unfortunately, there is no short cut to achieving an inner state in which you are able to consult your deep self whenever you need to. It takes sustained and focused work. But it can certainly be achieved. Knowing it is possible, in the way we have just discussed, is a necessary first step. Next you have to learn to focus and still your monkey mind. Then you have to work through the various negative and resisting behavioural traits that have shaped your current identity, and particularly its socialised self. Eventually you need to go even deeper and address other blocking essence level traits, including those that you have brought in from previous lives. All these interfere with establishing a connection between your everyday mind and your spiritual self. But as you eliminate those disruptive factors you enable a bridge to be built between your everyday self and your spiritual self. Eventually you'll be able to cross that bridge whenever you wish.

Of course, we are aware that building a bridge between the human and spiritual domains is a long-term task. It takes years. Right now it is perfectly effective for you to go into the quiet clearing within and seek confirmation of inner cues there.

As regards the difference between intuition and emotion, it all depends how you define those two words. If intuition is defined as an insight offered by the spiritual self, then such an insight may be sought when you are quiet and want to know something to do with your life circumstances. So a flash of insight or understanding emanating from your spiritual self may be called intuition in action. If you develop skill in becoming quiet and seeking such advice in the middle of the whirl of daily life, you may become open to spiritual level intuitive insights at any time.

In contrast, emotion occurs at the level of your socialised and essence selves. Both also provide their own flashes of insight. These kinds of emotional insight, such as a realisation about another's psychological state, or an instantly arrived at understanding of what led to that state forming, are often also called intuitions.

So, in practice, it can be said that there are both emotional and spiritual insights, and both are known as flashes of intuition. As with everything in the human domain, it can be difficult determining what level an insight has occurred on. Most people don't bother distinguishing between the emotional and spiritual, on the grounds that as long as there is insight that works, it's fine. This is valid. But deeper discernment between them is certainly possible.

What happens to me between lives?

What will happen to me between lives? How is my next life plan sorted, my next life selected, my future tasks identified? And how do I actually get reincarnated? How does the whole "between life process" work?

THE GUIDES RESPOND:

Life between lives cannot be entirely and adequately explained in terms available in the human domain. So our answer to this question will necessarily be indicative only, not full and complete. Nonetheless, we offer a serious and considered response.

As we have already stated, when a human being dies what dies is the body and the sub-identity associated with that body. All the sub-identity's experiences, including everything significant from the perspective of what was sought to be achieved in the life plan, and everything that supported and derailed the completion of the life plan, along with key moments and situations in which the individual was challenged or illuminated or gifted or transcended their socially constructed self, along with everything else not repetitively mundane, is uploaded to the individual's ongoing spiritual identity. This process occurs spontaneously because, of course, the ongoing spiritual identity is always "close by" its incarnated sub-identity.

In near death literature many stories are told of how after the body's death the individual awareness ascends to the so-called higher spiritual domain via a light, a tunnel, a staircase, or some other similar means. These descriptions are mental constructs, made by revived people who have attempted to describe, using their human mind and human imagery, what occurred to them when their awareness left its body and they underwent a near death experience. None of this actually happens in the way described in such literature. But these descriptions do offer a sound *indication* of the process involved. We suggest treating these stories as metaphors, not as literal descriptions.

The actual process—by which the deep spiritual self disengages from its now deceased body and simultaneously uploads experiential data to its own ongoing spiritual identity—is too complex to properly explain in human terms here. Rather than tie ourselves in knots attempting the impossible, let's just say it happens and move on.

As we described in an earlier response, every identity is part of a much larger group of spiritual identities. This larger group includes the equivalent of close and extended family members. On its return to the spiritual domain (we will use this metaphor, but remember it is a metaphor) the newly discarnated identity first refreshes itself by interacting with other identities to which it is close and who are not currently occupied with their own incarnation. Then it begins a process of reviewing what it experienced.

This review is much more immediate, visceral even, than human level reviews. The identity is able to relive each moment in all its complexity. But now being unencumbered by a human brain and its associated mind, and no longer embedded in a particular psychological makeup, the identity is able not only to relive the moment from the inside with striking lucidity, but can also review it from the perspective of all others who were involved. In effect, the reviewing process offers a 360 degree view of what occurred on all physical, psychological, emotional, intellectual and spiritual levels.

The review produces an accumulation of experiential data. Lessons are then extracted from that data. Just like on Earth, the lessons are extracted via self review, peer review and under the guidance of teachers. In the spiritual domain, teachers consist of more experienced identities. The purpose of reviewing and extracting lessons is to evaluate the essential activities of the life: what was done well, what wasn't done well, what was planned and achieved, what was planned and avoided, what was improvised and successfully pulled off, what was improvised and the individual fell flat on their face, and how they bounced back and continued living the life. All these are reviewed on multiple levels and lessons are extracted.

The lessons are derived in the context of what the identity set itself to achieve. Let's be clear about this. There is no yardstick any identity has to measure up to, no externally introduced scale that the identity is stood up beside and against which its successes and failures are evaluated. This does not happen. There are no rewards for succeeding brilliantly or punishments for screwing up royally. Both outcomes certainly happen with every single identity that incarnates in the human domain. We ourselves succeeded brilliantly at times and screwed up royally during our sequences of incarnations. That is the way learning occurs. However, the reviewing process takes place in an intimate, loving, nurturing environment, without judgement, and certainly without anything like human blaming and shaming.

In fact, the only one who is hard on the identity undergoing the review process is the identity itself. Because there is no hiding. Everything you do during your life, every subterfuge you engage in, every unsavoury (or savoury) feeling or action you hide from others' view, is exposed during the review process. Nothing significant remains unseen, either by the identity itself or by those other identities engaged in the review process.

One of the most common responses identities feel when they have completed their review is disappointment in themselves. They are disappointed they didn't make the most of opportunities that they themselves had planned to achieve. Or they are disappointed that when faced with a situation in which they needed to improvise, instead of drawing on facilities and abilities newly available to them they reverted to previous response patterns, patterns they were working on to adjust.

Of course, there is also elation, ecstasy even, in relation to those tasks that were successfully completed. But mostly, regarding those things that went well and were achieved at or beyond the anticipated level, there is a strong feeling of satisfaction.

Does this all sound very similar to human learning? Of course. Why does it? Because, as we stated earlier, the human domain is an extension of the spiritual domain. The opportunities created in the human domain are, at heart, spiritual opportunities, that is, opportunities for you, as a spiritual identity, to grow and evolve. In this sense human level learning reflects spiritual level learning, just on a narrower experiential base—for experience on the spiritual level is much fuller, much more immediate, much more vivid, much more real, to use that perhaps overworked and misunderstood term, than experience on the human level.

In a very real sense, embodiment involves "squeezing" a spiritual awareness into a human body and its associated mind. Not all of it can fit. So no spiritual identity is ever wholly and totally immersed and engaged in its human activities. Part of it remains in the spiritual domain. This is crudely expressed, but it indicates our point: right now you are simultaneously embodied and not embodied, simultaneously totally immersed in your current life and detached and free in the spiritual domain.

We don't mean to imply by this that what happens in the human domain doesn't matter. It absolutely does. You are living this life. It is real, with decisions and consequences for yourself and others, exactly as the spiritual domain is real. However, the two domains are real in different ways. And they are real for you in different ways. Can the human domain, then, be likened to a playground? Yes. But a very intimate and significant playground, just like a playground is real and immediate and important for a child, because its play is actually an opportunity to develop motor skills, social skills, where it learns to share, to care, to stick up for itself, and to be responsible for and to others. So much results from play because play is simultaneously frivolous and serious. Both those elements permeate your concurrent existence in the spiritual and human domains. With that somewhat enigmatic remark we will finish this aside and return to the central question.

Another activity that occupies identities between incarnations is further skill-building. Each identity has its natural propensities. It is attracted to certain types of activities over others. This same innate predilection is reflected during its incarnations on Earth, when it is attracted to certain occupations, professions and hobbies over others, because they naturally provide an opportunity for the identity to express its innate disposition. In the spiritual domain identities similarly engage in activities that resonate with them. They work on skills, and seek out further experiences, that facilitate their blossoming into who and what they wish to be.

All this is underpinned by personal choice. All identities decide for themselves what particular skill sets they wish to enhance, what domains of experience they wish to test themselves in, what outcomes they are striving after. But we note that choice generally occurs within the parameters set by the individual identity's innate disposition. Of course, all are free to attempt new tasks outside their current skill set and even beyond their personal disposition. Most prefer not to do so. But some do. As we keep repeating, choice reigns supreme.

Whatever skills are honed and whatever experiences are undergone between lives, these are then brought to the table, so to speak, when the goals and circumstances of the next life are considered. Part of the point of between life activities is to shore up weaknesses displayed during incarnation so you come back, to use sports jargon, bigger, better and stronger. In this sense, between life activities are like the training a sports person carries out between game days. Having worked on weaknesses on their game, sports people aim to re-enter the field of trial better equipped to handle the tests sports competition provides. The same applies to between life training.

As regards selecting what you will do in your next life, many, many factors are taken into account. The complexity of what is involved cannot be encapsulated in words, and certainly not in the brief responses such as we are making here.

What was previously said about intuition offers an insight into how the various factors are balanced when the next life is considered. In the human mind flashes of insight, called intuition, involve one, two or perhaps three factors coming into spontaneous alignment. A light then flicks on in your mind showing you in a wordless flash how these factors are connected. Take that moment of intuition and multiply it a thousand-fold. Then consider that this same thousand-fold flash is used to evaluate several options. That is the level of complexity that is involved when a next life scenario is evaluated.

What factors are involved in this evaluation? Numerous. In five books, collected under the heading of *The Spirituality Series*, we have explored (or intend to explore, as these books are currently still being written) many of the key factors involved in incarnation. For those readers who seek a much fuller explication of what is involved when the next life is selected, that series is recommended.

For now we will briefly say that what is selected involves a body and physical, family, social and cultural environments that will facilitate the identity achieving whatever tasks it has decided will occupy it this time round. Certain previously developed skills are also taken into the life, along with obstacle characteristics consisting of negative and self-limiting psychological traits. In addition, agreement is made to meet various spiritual friends. These you agree to work with or against, to love or fight, and to walk alongside for a long or short period. As we previously noted, the vast majority of these friends come from your close and extended spiritual family.

It might be asked, why would your spiritual friends agree to work against you or even fight with you? The answer is they agree to take on an adversarial role in order to challenge you and to force you to work hard and use your abilities to their maximum. Basically, adversarial roles provide you with the opportunity to, as is said in the vernacular, deal with your shit.

On the whole, those who challenge you at key junctures of your life, those who question what you are doing, those you push and probe you and try to persuade you to face up to your failings, are actually close spiritual friends. Who else would want to help you overcome weaknesses so your strengths may flower? Who else cares for you so much they would deliberately alienate themselves from you by rubbing you the wrong way but someone who loves you?

The lesson in what we have just asserted? Love those who ruffle you, who make you feel uncomfortable inside yourself. Don't react to them. Take on board whatever they are offering because it is a good, good opportunity generated by another who loves you dearly!

As regards the process by which a spiritual identity coalesces with a human foetus growing in its mother's womb, we have dealt with that elsewhere, particularly in *The Matapaua Conversations* and in *The Kosmic Web*. Those interested will find in those two books a theoretical description of the relationship between the spiritual and the physical, along with a detailed explanation regarding how a spirit remains embedded in a body.

This, then, is a potted history of what happens to an identity between one incarnation and the next. Of course, much else is involved. But this gives you a reasonably clear idea of what you'll be doing after this body dies and how you will go about preparing for your next incarnation.

Is more than one of me here right now?

So here I am in this life. When I shuffle off into the between life state to decide on my next life is all human history on the table? Can I return to this time now? Which would mean two of me would be living in the one time. Are there multiple versions of me occupying bodies in different parts of the planet right now? Is this how the relationship between the spiritual domain and the human domain works? Is this even possible?

THE GUIDES RESPOND:

This is one of those types of questions that fascinate some people, that they even become fixated on, because it involves such a conundrum. Can you be in the same place twice? Is the reality you live in, by which we refer to physical reality, more like lines of code as depicted in the film *The Matrix*, that will shatter when some great secret is learned? We'll respond on two levels, the level of your subjective experience, and our more detached abstract overview level.

For you, as a spiritual identity living in the middle of your experience of human existence in physical reality, information is largely given to you on a need to know basis. That is, as you come across a problem, or an issue, or you are seeking an explanation for what is happening to you or others in your life, you are drip fed information to help you make sense of what is happening. The source of this drip feeding reflects the sources that we described earlier in relation to who is watching over you. Information may additionally come from knowledgeable sources around you. For example, a book may contain the information you seek, or a particular specialist in a relevant field may become known to you. Simple enquiry at the level of the everyday mind, deliberately seeking knowledgeable sources, can discover much that is sought. This is because a great deal of information regarding all kinds of arcane matters is available, especially from sources that are slightly off the main road. Usually, it is the individual's own spiritual self that pushes an enquiry and draws attention to what otherwise might be passed by unnoticed. Of course, information is only discovered if it is actively sought. We observe your own spiritual self also knows a great deal, so it too may be consulted when you seek to make sense of aspects of your life.

Beyond these sources we have just identified—physical books, discussions with knowledgeable specialists, and consulting your own deep self—information may come from sources beyond you as an individual. Those in spirit who are watching over you may drip feed relevant information. These sources are, at the nearest level, those in your close and extended spiritual family. Then there are more experienced overseers and guides such as us. All these are repositories of an extensive collection of information, certainly far more than any single human brain can cope with.

This is why information is drip fed on a need to know basis. If everything you speculated about, every passing thought that passed through your mind, was responded to, you would be overwhelmed by such masses of information that it would end up being perceived as a disorganised mess. Accordingly, only information that directly helps you understand your current life circumstances is given to you.

We offer this as a general statement, because sometimes individuals do access information that is beyond their ability to make proper sense of. Some have gone mad as a result. Others have written or made statements that have elements of truth to them, but that aren't organised and related to other issues in a way that makes them coherent to others. Or, actually, to themselves. We refer here to individuals who have accessed the occult realm and its multiple sources of knowledge.

Accordingly, providing you, at the level of your everyday mind, access to the information you need at the time you need it is merely a common sense and practical approach to knowledge dissemination. It prevents a state of what, in common parlance, is referred to as "your mind being blown."

Drip-feeding information when and as you need it also ensures that you are able to integrate new information into what you already know. The new then becomes an addition to the established, it doesn't wreck the established altogether. Of course, new information may require you to abandon some parts of your existing beliefs sets, but this can be done in an orderly, non-explosive way. The intent is that outmoded knowledge simply gets dropped off as new knowledge arrives. In this way an individual's understanding grows in an entirely organic, natural way.

From your subjective perspective there is profitable enquiry and unprofitable enquiry. Profitable enquiry relates to facing your current life situation and seeking to understand what is happening in and behind it—by "behind" we mean the choices, deep connections, spiritual level intents and goals that have led to your current life situation coming to be. Unprofitable enquires involve investigations that not relevant to you understanding the who, what, here and why of your existence.

People with an active mind can and do become curious about all kinds of mysteries. Is there a UFO base on the dark side of the Moon? Is the government not telling you crucial facts? Is international finance being manipulated by a secret cabal? Or by snake-like aliens? Is the world about to go pop? People occupy themselves with all kinds of speculations about the nature of reality, what is going on in the human world, and what might be happening in other worlds. It is for this reason that conspiracy theories of all kinds abound. The way to approach this kind of mind distraction is as a bit of fun. It is a way to goof off and relax. As long as you don't take it too seriously, there's no problem. A problem does arise, however, when people become fixated on this speculative fluff and it distracts them from the proper business of their life. Then it interferes with them realising their life plan.

From your subjective experiential perspective, we suggest that wondering whether or not there is two of you living on this planet right now is such a distraction. It doesn't relate to what you need to address, which is the reality of your current life situation. So while we don't discourage such speculation, because it is certainly fun to let off a little steam by asking what if?, it is counterproductive to focus on it as a conundrum of reincarnation. There are much more important issues you need to address. At the risk of coming across like a party pooper, we encourage you to forget the fluff and focus on life's important stuff.

On the other hand, we do respect your right to ask such questions. So we will make a statement on the relationship between time and the spiritual domain that we hope will cast a little light on the stated conundrum.

From the spiritual realm, the physical dimension in which the Earth participates is a continuum that progresses from one state to the next. In this sense physical reality is sequential. This is also your human experience: you wake one morning, live that day, the end ends, you go to sleep, and that is that day complete. You then wake the next day and it is a new day, you live the new day, and so forth. As each day dies and another day is born, actions set into motion in one day have effects that manifest in the next day. So physical reality continues, with trails of actions and effects moving like spreading vines from one day, one month, one year, into the next.

From the spiritual dimension all points of that continuum are accessible simultaneously. But we make the caveat that this is not so for every being in the spiritual realm. Only when you have a sufficient overview, which any entity only begins to get when it has completed its incarnational cycle, does a full view of Earth's history become available. For identities who are still engaged in the reincarnational process, information is largely provided on a need to know basis. If a multiple-time view is required to help an individual make sense of their life plan, relevant information is provided.

We note, however, that identities who are engaged in their incarnational cycle do not see what is ahead for them. When they are considering their next life, possible outcomes are considered. But there is no definitive future, information about which is held back from them. Why is there no definitive future? Because each choice you make, each opportunity you take up or decline, shapes what you will become. There is no "final you", already in existence, which you are groping your way towards. The "future you" depends only and entirely on what you choose, moment by moment, to explore, take up or decline.

Speculation about the future is one of human beings' particularly futile lines of enquiry. All kinds of theories have been concocted in relation to predestination, God having decided, whether or not there is free will, and so on. Such speculation misses the point. You are a free agent who enters an ongoing physical reality life by life in order to evolve.

So incarnating individuals cannot access their own future states, because these future states do not yet exist. Yet all time is available to those with sufficient perspective. There is a conundrum here, in which the future exists but not future states for individuals. This conundrum cannot be resolved at the level of the human mind. Neither can it be resolved at the level of those disembodied spiritual identities who are still engaged in their reincarnational cycle.

Even for us, Earth's history exists more as a range of potentialities than as some kind of fixed frozen-in-spiritual-reality model. When we look at human history against the backdrop of the Earth, all the interactive complexity of which is playing out as a sequence that human beings call time, we see something that may be likened to an organic, living, moving, writhing, mass of snakes. The art is to enter into that mass and tease out tendrils, which represent, for the purpose of explanation, sequences of action and effect. This is, of course, a mere suggestion of how we perceive physical reality. And the perception is as mind-blowing as this image suggests.

As to the question of whether an individual identity can be incarnated on the planet in two different bodies simultaneously, we need to contextualise the question in order to respond. What happens is that, yes, an individual can select the same time more than once to incarnate into. For example, a certain period may be particularly conducive to developing particular skills and so the identity wishes to return to it in order facilitate their growth to the level of mastery. Occasionally, it may be a period that an individual has enjoyed and wishes to experience again, but this decision is actually infrequent. At the spiritual level you move on. Your focus is on more significant developmental issues rather than on having a good time in one particular corner of the globe. But it does happen.

So, yes, a single spiritual identity may occupy two bodies in the same time frame simultaneously. However, while incarnated the identity has no access to this knowledge. It is beyond an incarnating spirit's ability to access. By this we mean, spirits that are still incarnating have limited perception. Their perception in a disembodied state is, of course, far greater than what they possess while living inside a human body. But even between lives it is still limited.

This is why growing and evolving is so significant. We all go through experiences, absorb the lessons they provide, and feed our understanding as a result. With growth in understanding comes our personal evolution from naive and unknowing to knowing and loving. We expand. Our experiential base expands. Our ability to perceive expands. Our ability to process what we perceive expands. Our ability to put what we process into ever widening frames of reference expands. So progressively we perceive, appreciate, see ourselves as part of, and contribute to, what we previously were quite unaware of, that we didn't know even existed. This is clumsily put, but it is the truth.

So you, at your current level as an incarnating spiritual identity, experiencing and repeatedly returning to the corner of reality called Earth, can perceive, know and understand only a fraction of where you are. That is just the way of it. As you learn, as your understanding grows, and as you evolve as an identity, you will know ever more.

In the meantime, be a little humble. Recognise that, as is said, there is information out there that is "above your pay grade." But also know that as you grow and evolve your "pay grade" will rise too. Eventually, what is now a conundrum to you will be resolved. Or, as is often the case, you will come to realise your thinking was entirely askew and that reality is actually quite different to what you currently think.

When loved ones die is talking to them okay?

So what about grief? If a loved one isn't gone forever, if we're going to meet them again, I guess we should just nail the coffin and say, "See you later, matey"? But it's not that easy. We still grieve. Is grief okay? And what about communicating with the dead? Is it true we can feel them? Are there signs that the lost one is still around, that they're maybe even trying to influence us? Can they play hanky-panky with us? Can they influence us to make life choices because they know what is best for us to choose and do? Is it wise to seek their input? And if so, who can help us find and translate this information? Is it okay to do that, or is it wizardry, or even plain charlatanism?

THE GUIDES RESPOND:

Grief is a natural human emotion. As are desire, greed, self-pity, selfishness, and all the other emotions that give human existence its vitality and richness. Attempting to avoid a particular sensation, or suppress a particular feeling, because it isn't permitted according to some adopted frame of reference, some metaphysical scale, or some creed or set of rules, is counterproductive. You are here to engage in human reality in all its happy, sad and messy reality. So go to it.

However, the fact that the question asks whether grief is okay indicates something else is going on behind the question. Another question must be asked as to why is the person asking is uncomfortable about grief? What is the real underlying issue? Are there unresolved feelings in play, is there discomfort that things that should have been said and done were not before the deceased passed away? These are not questions we can answer. The enquiring individual must address them him or herself.

As a general statement, we would say that when a broad metaphysical or speculative issue troubles you, it is actually the tip of an iceberg of deeper concern. And the answer to the question is not to be found in abstract philosophic or metaphysical reasoning, but in the circumstances of your life. In effect, we recommend that whenever you have a big question of any kind, whenever some situation sticks out from the usual humdrum continuity of your life, whenever something creates a knot or blockage in the continuity of your everyday feelings and thought, treat it as a door. Open it up and use it enter into yourself. There you will find the deep question, along with the deep answer, to what troubles you.

As regards contacting the deceased, and whether they are still around, the answer is complex. Some deceased certainly do hang around the living. Usually this is because they are confused about what comes next, whether because they haven't gone through the reincarnational cycle many times before and so aren't familiar with the process, or because they have been told during their life that this or that will happen, and when it doesn't they become confused. It may be that during their life they were repeatedly told, and they came to believe, that they are nothing but a body. So when their body died, yet they found they were still conscious, they either didn't believe they were dead, or they became profoundly confused and didn't know what to do.

Many caught confused in this situation are so focused on the physical domain that they are unable, figuratively speaking, to look up and see the reality that stretches around them. So fixated are they on the physical that those in the spiritual domain are unable to attract their attention and invite them to enter what comes next. In such a situation only the physically living can help them out of their jam. And it is a jam, because they are caught between realms. It is like they are sitting in a drawer, a drawer that they have created entirely within their own mind, and they then shut the drawer, preventing contact by others. It takes the intervention of a physically incarnated identity to help them open the drawer and continue to the next phase.

Deep inside, the in-the-drawer individual knows this, too. They know there is somewhere else for them to be. They just need someone to give them a nudge so they trust what they already know. These jammed individuals often hang around those who can sense their presence. Psychics, and even family members with a little so-called sixth sense, become magnets for these discombobulated individuals.

Of course, not everyone knows how to respond when they feel a presence near them. What the confused deceased need is confirmation that they are dead, that they have no need to worry, and that their friends and family are waiting their arrival. This is usually enough for them to trust their own knowledge and happily open the drawer and set sail for what is next.

Another class of identities who may hang around the living are those newly deceased who are concerned that loved ones are missing them too much. They attempt to make contact to assure the so-called living that they are fine.

The love connection between individuals certainly continues into the between life state, and even into subsequent lives. As we previously observed, you repeatedly interact with members of your close and extended families. You may also form deep and abiding relationships with identities from far outside your extended family. These manifest in love relationships of all kinds: lovers, spouses, parents, children, lifelong friends, intensely committed work mates. Love relationships, in whatever forms they take, are often multi-life affairs. So where grief is the norm on the human level, ongoing love is the norm on the spiritual level.

Does this mean that you should consult psychics or mediums to make contact with deceased loved ones? Certainly do so if you feel you need to to deal with your grief, especially if you need confirmation that a loved one exists happily on another plane.

Does this mean that the freshly deceased can and do influence you in your current life? On the whole, no. Such an identity may join those who are already looking out for you and give you a nudge, or a wake up call, or provide required information, from time to time, so you may complete tasks and realise your life plan. If others are not getting through to your everyday mind and making the sought impact, they may enlist the services of the freshly deceased, to whom you have opened yourself up, to provide what is needed. This happens.

But in general the freshly deceased have their own work to do in the between life state, as we described in the previous response. So they are too preoccupied to make an effort to influence you. And anyway, as we just said, any influence is only ever in accordance with what you need in your embodied state, not what they are exploring in their disembodied state.

As to hanky-panky, yes, mischievous spirits do exist. These are identities with some experience who have learned how to manipulate physical objects while in a disembodied state. They use their skills to hang around the embodied and create various kinds of local mayhem. There are varying degrees of maliciousness involved, but such individuals don't have the power to create widely dangerous and significant mayhem. Basically, these situations require an embodied individual with sufficient perception to notice them and draw the attention of helpers in the spiritual domain to what is happening. They will then shift on the mischievous spirit and clear the local area.

Most people are completely unaware of what is happening around them in the interface region between the physical and spiritual. Some identities take on the task of developing skills to help those who are stuck or who are deliberately hanging around. Such abilities are called psychic. While they all get lumped under the one banner, psychics actually have different skill sets. Some are good at connecting the living with the deceased, others see so-called ghosts and auras, some are health oriented, yet others have insight into future possibilities. Psychics also vary in the levels of their expertise. Some are just starting out, others have been honing their skills for several lives. Some exaggerate their abilities. All tend to have certain personality quirks and weakness they are still working through. This means that while psychics have an advanced skill set in one part of themselves, in other parts they are just an ordinary person, manifesting the same negativities, uncertainties, over-boldness, and fears that everyone has.

Accordingly, when consulting a psychic, use your own discernment. Certainly, the psychic who exaggerates, or who even lies about their abilities, is not doing so in a vacuum. Others want them to be what they are pretending to be. So, as you need to with everything in the human world, use your discernment. If consulting a psychic is an experience you want, certainly do it. But do so with your eyes open, feelings slightly held back, and mind alert.

Question 16

Does collective sorrow have a deeper purpose?

I realise that sorrow is an emotion people feel individually. But is there a collective sorrow, as occurs when we hear of someone we don't know passing and feel grief? Tragic natural disasters caused by tsunamis, hurricanes and famines also create widespread sorrow. Is there such a thing as collective sorrow and does it have a purpose?

THE GUIDES RESPOND:

We'll begin by differentiating between sorrow and self-pity. Self-pity, like associated emotions such as depression and despair, is self-focused. It has to do with one's personal response to life circumstances and to one's own inner state. In contrast sorrow, at least in the way we are interpreting this question, is outwardly directed. It involves having sympathy for others. But, beyond this, sorrow involves a gentle, honeyed, bitter feeling about life and what happens in it.

When an individual feels sorrow in the face of others' misfortunes, that is a sign of maturity. It is a sign that they are able to get out of themselves, out of their mundane daily concerns, and adopt a wider, more selfless perspective. Of course, such a feeling can quickly concertina down into a self-focused, woe-is-me feeling more akin to self-pity. But that doesn't invalidate the original sorrowful feeling.

Collective sorrow is an unusual state. It usually takes an extraordinary person—recent examples are Nelson Mandela and Princess

Diana—to galvanise public emotions in this way. In asserting this we are aware that, like everyone else, these two individuals were certainly flawed. But in their lives they came to represent many people's higher aspirations for what it is possible to achieve. When these sub-identities of two ongoing spiritual identities died, the sorrow that was so widely felt had two main intertwined emotions.

One was a regret that they had died, that they were no longer around to inspire others to higher, more caring and universally nurturing accomplishments. The other much more subtle factor, was a recognition that what they represented is available to all, but that individuals in their own lives, and humanity as a whole, is failing to achievement it. This is where the slightly bitter flavour comes in. The sweetness has to do with acknowledging higher possibilities, and the regret arises due to recognition that those possibilities are not manifest in the world. Thus sorrow becomes a mixture of sweetness and a subtle acrid favour.

When people feel sorrow, it is a direct manifestation of their spiritual self. That is, the sorrow itself, while experienced at the level of everyday emotion, is actually experienced much more deeply. So when masses of people together experience sorrow, it is a rare occasion when large numbers of incarnated identities are aligned at the spiritual level. Such an alignment is a rare event.

It is an irony of human existence that such an alignment occurs in the context of tragedy, such as when a disaster leads to sudden or massive loss of life, or when a significant individual passes on. The same universally shared alignment occurs much less frequently in moments of joy.

Examples of joyous events, certainly shared by millions but not by all, include when a new religious leader, such as a Pope or Dalai Lama, is appointed. Such appointments are significant at a deep level because they bring together many people's hopes and aspirations of the world. The first election to office of President Obama fostered a similar collective feeling of hope and joy that the world could become different.

Of course, such heroes usually fall rapidly, because the hopeful want them to magically transform the world. This is an impossible hope. Transforming the world requires collective effort. No single person will ever achieve it. So when the individual fails, which is inevitable, disappointment, followed by bitterness and cynicism, creep back in and the hero is blamed for failing to achieve what they were never going to.

In this sense sorrow is an emotion that lingers longer than hope. Both emotions have to do with people projecting their deepest aspirations onto another person, who then becomes a figurehead or a symbolic representation of humanity's highest qualities. But hope is always shown to be misplaced, because the individual onto whom people have projected their hope is still alive to remind everyone that they have failed. Whereas those whose passing stimulated sorrow continue to live in the mind, often sustained by public rituals and commemorations, perhaps for generations. So they linger as a symbol who focuses the best of human aspirations.

Collective sorrow, like collective hope, reflects the shared aspirations of multiple aligned spiritual identities. As such both function as significant reminding factors of the heights that may be achieved in the human domain, heights that reflect the depths present within each individual incarnated identity.

That collective sorrow occurs just now and then, as events and individuals come and go, is sufficient. It serves its purpose of reminding all of what they as individuals, and humanity as a whole, may eventually become.

Question 17

Does my pet have a soul?

When I look at my dog he really does seem to be looking back at me. My cat also responds to what is going on, interacts with me and others, and communicates what it wants, when it wants it. All this suggests pets have something going on inside them. Is this the case? Is there a spiritual element within animals? Does my pet have a soul?

THE GUIDES RESPOND:

Human beings are socially conditioned to think of themselves as superior to other living creatures. They are especially conditioned to think they have a soul where other creatures don't. This is totally erroneous.

All animals and plants have a soul of some kind, although the relationship between the spiritual and physical components of different creatures varies in the kinds of souls they possess and in the types of connections that exist between that soul and its corresponding body. So there is no one-size-fits-all explanation that can adequately answer this question. In addition, explaining everything involved would take many more words than we have at our disposal in these brief forays into matters spiritual. Nonetheless, we will answer as clearly as we can.

First, we need to address the use of the word "soul." This word is somewhat vague and, for our purposes, has unnecessary religious connotations. Our preference is to talk of spirits as identities. That is, each "thing" existing in the spiritual domain is best referred to as an identity. Identities possess many qualities: intellect, an ability to love, a continuing sense of its own self no matter what spiritual or physical environment it is in, and a sense that some identities with which it interacts are more experienced, attuned and skillful than it is, while other identities it meets are less so. Through experience and by degrees each identity also learns that other identities, in their intrinsic natures, are not as it is. There is no denigration or praise involved in this differentiation. It is simply a matter of fact: spiritual identities come in many different kinds, and each identity has its own particular set of sensitivities, skills and desires with respect to what it seeks to do and the goals it sets itself to achieve.

We say all this as a preamble to the discussion of pets, because different pets are, or perhaps it is more accurate to say different pets *embody*, a variety of quite different spiritual identities. In order to give this discussion a context and so ensure it is useful to you, we'll comment a little on human spiritual identities.

You, as a spiritual identity, are a fragment of a much larger entity. As we stated earlier, you are one of somewhere between, on average, 800 and 1200 separate fragments. What we mean by this is that when you came into existence, that is, when you were created out of that undifferentiated consciousness that could be called God (to utilise that somewhat overused and misconceived word), you were at first part of a much larger spiritual entity. Some period after it came into existence that entity split into approximately one thousand fragments. You, as an individual identity, are just one among those individual fragments. You continue to associate closely with many among this thousand or so fragments because they are, literally, your intimate family. They support you in your efforts, and you naturally support them.

The reason your overall entity fragmented was so it could experience, learn and evolve. Having one thousand fragments of consciousness exploring complex and rich spiritual and physical realms allows for the accumulation of a huge amount of experiential information that includes physical manoeuvrings, emotional exchanges and intellectual explorations. These experiences facilitate the growth of multi-layered understanding.

Once you and your family of spiritual fragments have explored the physical domain and learned all you wish to, you will coalesce back into your original single entity. But when you do so that entity will be enriched by the experiences of a thousand or so fragments bringing a million plus human lives worth of experience. At the completion of all its fragments' incarnation cycles, the entity will be vastly more knowing and loving than it was when it was initially created. It will have evolved to a much more complex state of sensitivity than when it began. It will be stronger and possess skills it couldn't even dream of in its initial naive state. All this coalesces during reintegration at the end of all the fragments' reincarnation cycles.

Each fragment's reintegration process itself begins towards the end of its reincarnation cycle and occurs over a number of lives. Reintegration involves learning to live with others on Earth and loving them in a quite selfless manner. It also involves the fragment using the periods between this final sequence of lives to compare notes and resolve issues that have arisen throughout all its incarnated lives. Learning not to be an individual, and especially absorbing all the lessons around reintegrating your awareness into a host of others, is a complex, somewhat fraught activity. But it can and always is done—as we ourselves, your guides in this, can attest to.

All this encompasses the process of experiencing and learning that is appropriate for spirits who utilise human bodies and human social interactions to evolve. But this is not the pattern for all spiritual identities. Some, such as those who occupy horses and canines, utilise a similar pattern of fragmenting, occupying animal bodies, and using the experience to evolve. Others, such as those which utilise the experience of cats, utilise a quite different process. A little detail will clarify this. Let's begin with dogs.

Those spiritual entities that utilise the canine experience split into a smaller number of fragments than do those identities that utilise the human experience. On average they number between 60 and 150 fragments. This is indicative only, as some entities fragment to a greater extent and others to a lesser. But these numbers provide an average range.

The nature of these fragments differ from the fragments that occupy human beings. However, as many pet owners will attest, love, devotion, tenderness, and care are all qualities present in those fragmented identities that inhabit the various canine species. It is also clear that at times instinctive self-protective animal traits manifest in dogs, so rage, violence, sexual urges, an ability to identify friends and threats via smell, and so on, naturally dominate the awareness of individual dogs. Socialisation also impacts on the canine awareness, so trust and distrust, encouraged helpfulness to others and encouraged greed, manifest in the behaviour of individual canine animals.

All this means that the dog awareness is layered similarly to how a human awareness is layered, with animal and instinctive urges, socialised behaviours, and an underlying spiritual identity, all manifesting in any individual doggy identity. Also like human beings, the spiritual fragments that incarnate in dogs do so repeatedly as they seek to experience, learn and evolve. The exact numbers of incarnations differ between species, with some incarnating dozens, others hundreds of times.

The reason for these differences is that canine minds differ in complexity between species. Some doggy brains are rich and complex, especially emotionally, while others are less so. Accordingly, different complexities of spiritual identities enter different canine species, with the more complex fragments entering species with more complex brains, and those that are less complex entering species with less complex neurology.

For the same reason more complex fragmented identities incarnate more times because they are able to absorb a wider variety of experiences and at a greater depth. So they obtain more from their successive incarnations. In this way a spiritual fragment enriches itself and has more to bring back and contribute to its overall identity when the fragments recombine.

We would note that within the canine world a very wide range of experiences is available. The life of domesticated canine is most common, but domestication extends from a working dog on a farm to that of a pampered pooch that spends its life entirely inside. There is a life in wild as a wolf, or a different kind of life in the wild in urban streets. There are dog experiences of being abused, of being loved, of losing those the dog loves and who love the dog, of grieving, of getting over grief, of forming new relationships. And, as with human beings, there is the experience of being overwhelmed by animal instincts and of engaging in the process of learning how to regulate instincts within the overall multi-layered doggy awareness.

As regards spiritual cognition, during any incarnation dogs are never aware that they are a fragment of an ongoing spiritual identity. This marks a difference between the quality of awareness of spiritual fragments that occupy human bodies and those that occupy canine bodies. This, we must point out, does not mean that one type of fragment is superior to another. It just demarcates a difference in fundamental nature.

Of course, there are other kinds of spiritual identity who maintain a much greater awareness of their spiritual identity while embodied than those who incarnate in human bodies do. In this sense, they are more complex fragments than you are and we were. We note, there are none such incarnating on this planet. They occupy bodies in other parts of the multiverse.

We state all this merely to illustrate a point: there is no basis for human beings to get bigheaded or filled with ideas of superiority. A range of complexity exists among spiritual fragments and spiritual identities. You are neither the simplest or the most complex form of identity. You are merely one variety among an extensive range. So the conditioned human sense of superiority to other species on this planet, and the sense that the human is closer to God than any other identity, is simply wrong. We advise all to readjust their outlook to accommodate this fact. Pet lovers, of course, already know this through their personal experience, even though they are unlikely to describe what they know in quite these terms.

We will offer one more example of the varieties of spiritual identities, this in relation to another common pet, the cat. As is clear to pet owners, cats are less emotionally complex than dogs. Their brains are smaller, their neocortex and limbic systems are simpler, and they tend to be even more wholly dominated by their instinctive impulses than dogs are. Accordingly, correspondingly less complex spiritual identities are associated with cats. Nonetheless, as with all identities, they use their entry into the feline domain to experience, learn and evolve.

The usual combination of instinctive impulses, socialisation and an expression of the ongoing spiritual identity applies. Pet owners will know that, just as with dogs and human beings, some cats manifest more personality and convey a sense of possessing greater inner depth. Some cats are more sociable, others are more jittery, yet others prefer solitude. All seek to communicate to a greater or lesser extent with those around them. Such manifestations reflect the growth of the identity that is associating with the individual cat.

As far as the ongoing spiritual identity's relationship to the individual cat is concerned, this is different to the way a fragment occupies an individual dog. The identity that associates with cats isn't a fragment in the way that applies to canines and humans. A cat's spiritual identity is always a whole. Furthermore, it doesn't occupy a feline body serially, one at a time, but instead extends its awareness into several cats simultaneously. So where an identity who occupies a dog obtains its richness of experience through sequentially exploring doggy social, instinctive and emotional interactions, and much of those with human beings, the identity that occupies cats obtains its richness of experience through breadth, experiencing across a range of animals at the same time.

This is not at all what you as an owner would perceive in the pet you call yours. Of course, ultimately there is no ownership involved. There is only a period during which you interact with another kind of spiritual identity through the relationship you forge with your pet. And, like any relationship, that incorporates loving, nurturing, teaching, communicating, and sharing your time together.

Does this relationship extend beyond the death of your bodies? In many cases, yes. However, there is rarely an ongoing multi-life relationship. If you wish you may organise to reincarnate with a favoured spiritual identity that adopts animal form. But ultimately you and your pet are taking very different trajectories through all the varieties of experiences offered by incarnation on this planet. So extended associations do not occur.

What is the point, then, of raising and caring for pets? Simply, pets present an opportunity to conduct a relationship with another identity that is less complex and demanding than normal human interactions. Many people find this a comforting, even satisfying experience. Be assured, those beings you call your pets do too.

Question 18

Does a hierarchy exist in the spiritual realm?

Your comments on pets, that spiritual identities have differing levels of complexity, suggests there is some kind of hierarchy. Is this the case? Is there an order of being in the spiritual domain? And is this order organised hierarchically into higher and lower? When anyone channels messages, does this hierarchy play a role in relation to where the message comes from?

THE GUIDES RESPOND:

This question brings us to another situation in which language derived from the human social perspective cannot adequately reflect what occurs in the spiritual domain. The best we can do is respond to this question regarding hierarchy by saying, yes. And no. We'll explain.

Spiritual identities have different degrees of complexity. Just as an amoeba is a less complex organism than a bird, and a bird is less complex than a human being, there are many different varieties of spiritual identity possessing different kinds of sensitivities and different kinds of innate abilities. In fact, there are far greater varieties of spiritual identities than the combined number of species that have once, do now, or ever will, cohabit on Earth. So among spiritual identities there is a wide range of ability, capacity, intention and goals.

However, on Earth differences in complexity lead to an inability to communicate. Amoeba, birds and human beings can never have deeply meaningful exchanges of information. Differences between their biological, neural and cognitive organisations stops communication occurring. In the spiritual realm no such barrier to communication or information exchange exists. So differences in complexity do not isolate identities in the way that species are isolated on Earth. This also means spiritual identities are not arranged into orders of hierarchy as they are on Earth.

The notion of hierarchy is a human social construct. Human beings look at other creatures around them, observe that they do not have language or culture as human beings do, perceive that other species cannot construct with the complexity and precision that their opposed thumb enables, and recognise that there is nothing on the planet to rival human achievement. So human beings place themselves at the top of the tree of life and situate all other creatures as lower. Which means, ultimately, human beings view all other species as lesser.

Within human social organisation this idea of greater and lesser is basic. Some people are called greater because of their bloodline, or their wealth, or because they are able to do more than is usual with their bodies, emotions or minds, or simply because they are popular. Others are called lesser on the same grounds. Individuals are especially identified as lesser when they do not have a fully functioning body or brain, so lack a capacity everyone else naturally has.

This higher-lower hierarchy is crucial not just to human social relations but also to how human beings act in the world. In particular, human beings use their self-granted higher status to justify exploiting or eradicating other species according to their desire. Religion reinforces this notion of greater status by having God name humanity the highest of all creation and granting humanity rights over everything in the physical domain.

What all this adds up to is that when human beings look out into the cosmos and seek to understand things they only tangentially perceive, they naturally draw on their same sense of social hierarchy and status. In this situation human notions around hierarchy are simply inappropriate. We repeat, the spiritual domain is not organised hierarchically. How, then, is it organised?

As we have said elsewhere, instead of notions of hierarchy and status we prefer to use the idea of complexity. Different entities have different degrees of complexity. Yet all entities are able to interact equally. How, then, do differences in complexity impact on their interactions? To use another human notion—and human notions are all we *can* use to express perceptions that hover at the edge of human expression—different entities possess varying degrees of sensitivity to the layers of information encoded into communications. You may want to read this last sentence more than once.

To give this somewhat abstract statement concrete form, it is like when two people listen to a car engine running. Both can hear a slight clank, indicating a problem. But the experienced mechanic hears more, or to be more precise, can extract more information from the same sound, than can the other who is not trained in motor mechanics. Of course, training comes down to knowledge, experience and the continued practical application of what is learned. So the untrained person can choose to become a trained mechanic and so become aware of what the trained hear but that the untrained do not.

In saying this we are referring to evolution. All identities evolve. So a significant issue on the spiritual level is that one identity may be naive and inexperienced and the other experienced and wise. So naturally there is a difference in sensitivity between them. Does this make one better or higher than the other? Of course not. It just means they are at different stages in their growth cycles.

In addition, different identities possess inherently different capacities. Some identities are sensitive in ways not available to other kinds of identities. So within their growth cycles some identities cultivate certain sets of sensitivities and abilities, while others cultivate different sensitivities and abilities. Does this mean some are better or higher or more valuable than others? No. They are just different.

As to the question regarding orders of being, once again the answer is yes and no. Yes, there are orders of being, which may be categorised in the same way that biological organisms are separated into different families, divisions, species and so on. But this is simply a fact of existence. If you have an intellect and wish to use it to first identify different types of beings, then divide those identities into categories and sub-categories, that is entirely possible. But doing so does not imply that you are recognising a pre-existing hierarchy. It is an intellectual exercise, nothing more. Taking the next step, as human beings do, and giving status and value to various self-identified categories and sub-categories does not occur on the spiritual level.

However, we will say that there is a case to be made that, to use a human commonplace, birds of a feather flock together. Identities that have the same intrinsic nature do tend to interact together, particularly when they compare notes about their existence and what they have experienced, and when they strive to make sense of those experiences. When you are learning any task it is useful to associate with others who are teaching and learning that same task. This is just common sense. You keep to those who are learning like you because that is the best and fastest way to absorb all the nuances involved.

So while reality is teeming with all kinds of spiritual identities, and while reality definitely offers an infinitely extensive range of experiences, a freshly evolving identity doesn't dart from one to the other, tasting this, leaping into that, trying something else. Most identities focus on the immediate task at hand. For those incarnating in human bodies, that involves using incarnation to become more sensitive, to overcome fear and crude reactivity, to learn how to adjust awareness in a range of pleasant, trying, horrifying and intoxicating situations, and through all this evolve their identity and their capacity to cope no matter what is happening to them. The goal is that once human existence has been gone through, you, as an individual identity, and especially as an identity that has reintegrated back into its overall multi-fragment entity, has evolved into a situation in which whatever is out there to be experienced may be negotiated with huge sensitivity, using self-possessed awareness and manifold capacities.

Among what will be encountered, some identities possess a complexity vastly greater than even an entity made up of its reintegrated fragments. Other identities are much less complex. Others are just of another order altogether. But throughout all encounters notions of hierarchy as understood in the human domain will be non-existent. Other concerns occupy our attention, as it will yours when you come to be where we are now—but in your own way, of course.

Could we present a demarcation between the orders of being that exist in the spiritual realm? We could. But we won't. This is beyond our brief. We will limit what we identify to interactions that occur within the human field of spiritual experience. And we won't do so here but in other publications, some already written, others yet to be produced. If you are interested in learning more we direct you to those books, articles and statements.

Our use of the phrase "beyond our brief" has surely intrigued you. We bring that notion to this discussion in relation to the final part of this question: Does hierarchy play a role in relation to messages, channelled or otherwise, that manifest from the spiritual domain into the human realm?

We are functioning in accordance to a wider intention. It is an intention that includes us but that extends beyond us to include other identities. These identities have more experience and are more extensively and deeply evolved than us. That wider intention currently places restrictions on what is being communicated. But there is nothing covert in this. We are not holding back secrets. It is simply another matter of common sense.

Any teaching situation has a teaching plan. This is a strategy that identifies the material that needs to be communicated, establishes a sequence by which material will be imparted, and generates exercises and tests to ensure each student has internally consolidated what has been taught. The whole teaching-learning process has a progression, so the next set of information naturally builds on what has gone before. A teacher does a student no good by imparting material from the end of the course at the beginning of the course. The student will have no way of contextualising the advanced information. Preliminary steps need to taken, and an orderly progression made, for the student to get the most out of what is imparted.

Exactly the same process applies to the sharing of spiritual knowledge. Information has to be imparted progressively. Truths can be stated today in a way that could not be offered ten thousand years ago. Human culture, sensitivity to social interactions, and the complexity of information itself, have developed. Of course, we are not implying this current situation is better in a judgmental sense. Cultural evolution has certainly taken place as more people work through their cycles of incarnations. But counterbalancing the progress is much that is less than optimal. Yet that will also be smoothed out and brought to a higher level as everyone becomes more experienced in the game that is being human.

So, to return to the question, we are working in harmony with a wider intent. We impart information in an orderly fashion. The exact progress that is made is dependent on how those we are teaching absorb their lessons. Note, however, that the time frame within which we are working is not a human yearly teaching-learning cycle, or even a multi-year university degree cycle. Rather, the time frame involves hundreds of years. This is why, at this time, we are providing information within certain parameters. As lessons are learned the parameters will expand. But much has yet to be imparted, learned and absorbed before that will occur.

Furthermore, the brief we are working to has been imparted to us as an intent, not in a form anything like a human teaching or action plan. Does this mean we are functioning within some kind of spiritual hierarchy? It is certainly the case that we are working ("working" is another human word that is close to, but doesn't quite capture, the nature of what we are doing) with identities that are more experienced than we are. However, we are not "below" them in a human hierarchical sense. Our relationship is akin to what occurs between responsible adults. To explain.

In the human social arena people are organised into various hierarchical categories. One principal hierarchy is between child and adult, with the adult being superior and having the status to command and organise the child. Another hierarchy is organised according to pay grade, with those who are paid more having authority over those who are paid less. Now imagine a scenario in which everyone involved is a self-responsible adult and there are no pay grades. That offers something of a taste as to how we function in a multiple identity context in which many are "working" with a unified intent.

These messages from the so-called spiritual realm sent into the human domain are offered with love and much goodwill. We wish you to succeed in understanding the reality of what you are experiencing, how you came to be where you are, why you are there, and what is the best way of taking advantage of your current situation. But, at the same time, you are simply unable to comprehend all the reality that is involved. Just by virtue of your incarnated state, you are unable to comprehend where we are and what order of being we partake of. But that will not always be so. Take your baby steps in understanding. And as your wisdom grows you will be able to take greater and greater steps ... until one day you will walk among the stars.

Question 19

Is life a game? Are we the butt of a cosmic joke?

In various answers you have compared human existence to games. You began by comparing our life to a fun fair. In the last response you referred to "the game that is being human." Elsewhere you have evoked the image of children in a playpen. What is behind these statements? Is reality just some kind of playground? Are we even living a joke existence, as cynics suggest? Are we the butt of a cosmic joke?

THE GUIDES RESPOND:

We have introduced this imagery for one simple reason: human beings take all this spiritual stuff too seriously! By this we mean too earnestly, too heavily. Humanity has turned spirituality into religion and religion into a burdensome set of commands that are strapped across children's shoulders and weigh them down for the rest of their lives!

When religion is taught in any circle it involves a number of related issues, particularly instilling a sense of personal inadequacy, guilt, rules, obligations, and restrictions, not just as to what can be done but as to what is allowed to be delved into and explored. Religion especially involves a series of big NOs: You can't do this, you can't do that, you can't say or think this, you can't say or think that.

In addition, all religions push the big button of fear. Fear is what cripples you. Fear stops you realising your true worth. Fear keeps you in the corner, too scared to do what you really want. The fact that fear is the big driver in all religions is the greatest argument for shrugging off the strictures of religion. There is no spiritual reality that the big NOs of religion reflect.

On the other hand, some among the YESs pronounced by religions do correspond to human spiritual reality, for example, the religious push to be considerate of others. But you don't have to be a member of a religion to consider others.

In fact, the YESs of religion fall into two categories: mutually beneficial and fantastical. The mutually beneficial manifests in all human societies. It is seen in communal living, in how people band together to feed themselves, build shelters, raise children, give children an education, and look after the aging. This is all basic human consideration and love. No one needs a religious finger tut-tutting over them to carry out such acts. People willingly, contentedly even, do all these. Why? Not for religious reasons. Simply because they are expressions of human love.

The fantasy YESs offered by religions consist of such notions as heaven and the promise that true believers will sit for eternity with angels and saints, even God, or alternatively will live on a spiritual planet somewhere, forever and placidly content. Let us assure you, there is no sitting around in the so-called afterlife. The between life period is full and busy.

You are an immature but growing identity. To use a humorous metaphor, between lives you need feeding and burping. The feeding involves helping you process what you have experienced and transforming it into valuable nutritious psycho-spiritual material that fuels your growth. The burping involves helping you get over what you have choked on during your last life, and what during the between life period you continue to uneasily process.

None of this is a joke. It is real. It involves your personal evolution. On the other hand, there is no reason you can't have fun throughout the entire process.

Human beings tend to adopt extreme positions. So the sombre religious see life as a battle for their immortal soul, and their least screw up will condemn them to hell for all eternity. This is the ultimate fear that religions use to cower believers. Alternatively, the cynical see religion as humbug. Perceiving the often bizarre meanings human beings generate to explain their existence, cynics react extremely by viewing all human searches for meaning as bogus. They then conclude that life is a mere accident and suggest that the cosmos, in giving human beings self-awareness, is even playing a huge joke on everyone. Neither of these extreme perspectives reflects reality.

Given that these are positions that human beings actually adopt, our response to this situation is two-fold. First, we are attempting to provide some common sense responses to arcane questions regarding humanity's spiritual nature, and to do so without coercing you into anything, and especially without pushing the fear button. Second, we wish to foster some lightheartedness about it all.

Each life is about exploration, trying things out, having a go. Fear interferes with that. We encourage you not just to shrug off the fears that others seek to project onto you, but also, and this is even more important, we encourage you to work against your own deeply buried fears.

Sometimes a whim that passes through your awareness, that you shrug off thinking, "No, I can't do that!", has more to it. Sometimes it is an expression of a deep urge that seeks expression, something you are in a position to try now, in this life, that you haven't been in a position to try in any prior life. Listen out for deep urges. They have the potential to lead you into entirely new regions of your self.

The image of children in a playpen or schoolyard learning by playing, offered in earlier responses, was deliberately chosen. Children take each day as it comes. They are not initially burdened by big DO NOTs. However, as children grow adults continuously force many DO NOTs onto them. While some are common sense—such as not touching hot things—many are projections of fear. Current examples are the pressure being put on the young to start saving and investing for their retirement, and the religiously projected fear that they need to invest in church beliefs otherwise God will reject and abandon them for eternity.

We don't suggest you try returning to the state of being a child. You can't do so. You know too much. But we do suggest that you cast off adopted fears and that you inwardly alter your attitude towards life so that you see each day as a fresh opportunity to engage, to live, to be. Play the game of being human with zest, with appetite, with verve.

There is no need to plod heavily. Dance lightly. Life isn't a burden. It's a joy. Even in the middle of your darkest moments there are glimpses out through the window of the sky, of flitting birds, of trees and mountains. Nothing is forever. Love. Learn. Be.

Question 20

Do we each have a personal guide?

You keep referring to us being observed and guided. People talk about each of us having an individual guide. Is it true that we have our own personal guide (or guides) who are with us all the time? If so, do we keep the same guides with us through all our lives?

THE GUIDES RESPOND:

A big part of playing involves other people. As we indicated earlier, when children play with others in a sand pit a range of skills are involved, including physical dexterity, interpersonal skills in dealing with other children, confronting personal desires and modifying them to the social context, developing language skills to communicate, and so on. Play is not just important to kids, it is vital to their growth. Play is serious fun!

Sports are an example of adult play. Of course, many play sport professionally, for money. But at heart it remains another form of serious fun. Each player has to work on personal physical fitness and dexterity, absorb the game plan, communicate with their team mates, adjust their desires to fit with the team culture, learn to deal with coaches and trainers, get the best out of themselves and others, and fire themselves up for repeated competition. As such, sport isn't a metaphor for life as a seriously fun game for adults, it *is* the game of life for adults.

Without multiple individuals working, thinking, feeling and achieving, without multiple individuals *playing together*, there is no game of life. Multiple individuals interacting implies a multiplicity of roles. In a sports team there are the defenders, the attackers, the star players, the workhorse team players, the show ponies, those who are struggling for form, the rehabilitating, the newbies who want to make their mark, the oldies who are nearing retirement and wondering what to do next.

Then there are all the coaches, including the defence coach, the attack coach, the head coach, the video analyst, the nutritionist, the yoga coach, the psychologist who works with players on attitude and headspace. And that's not forgetting the role played by the opposition teams who are striving to win and so negate, at least in terms of the competition ladder, what all these different individuals in the teams they play against are collectively working to achieve.

So within the game of life there are multiple roles. There is also much switching of roles. The head coach was once a player. The fitness trainer may have wanted to be a pro player but never possessed enough physical presence or skill. The physiotherapist may love bringing the science of anatomy to a sports team. The star player who is about to retire may want to become a referee. Or a sports administrator. Or a commentator. Or any of the many team-related roles.

So in sports there are multiple roles and individuals switch between them. This equally applies to the game of life. Or, to be more exact, the game of multiple incarnations. In one life you're a trainer. In another you're a player, In yet another you're a coach. You may repeat each role a number of times until you've got it down. Then you move onto another field of activity that attracts you, that furthers what you have learned by allowing you to apply what you have just learned in new contexts.

What we are getting at is that no one has just one role, even within a single lifetime. Roles shift, metamorphise, evolve, transform into something else completely. The same applies spiritually. You play the game of life with other identities. And across lives you all exchange roles. The result is that at the end of a sequence of lives you know that particular field of human activity inside out.

This is all by way of a preamble to answering the question: Do I have a personal guide who continues life after life? As will be clear from what we have just stated, roles change. So the brief answer is no, you do not have a single personal guide who oversees your full range of incarnations. On the other hand, you do have single guides who oversee specific aspects during a sequence of incarnations. They have expertise relevant to what you are doing. They help you achieve expertise. And when you learn what you wish to they move on. Let's expand on this a little more.

Every spiritual identity is learning particular sets of skills that are directly related to their fundamental nature, that are creative expressions of their innate disposition. Let's say one person has a servant disposition. Their overall bliss is to support others as they engage in the game of life. But support comes in innumerable forms. This person may focus on nurturing small children. Or prefer working with adults, helping them get through tough patches. Or is attracted to childbirth, or organising groups, or feeding the team. All these, and many, many other activities, are separate expressions of the intent to nurture.

Through a thousand lives, this identity possessing a servant disposition will engage in and develop expertise in many of these roles, although they will likely specialise in particular sets of related roles, such as those that nurture the young, or with the process of transitioning teens from one situation to another. As this identity changes specialities it will have various mentors—perhaps a more appropriate term than guides—who through personal experience have developed their own expertise in particular kinds of nurturing. Sometimes these mentors will incarnate with the individual to act as a human mentor, or as a human patient, as a supportive spouse, and even as a personal or professional adversary. The adversarial role is important because it serves to challenge and push, the aim being to ensure the individual concerned doesn't just repeat what they have previously done but is forced to confront and overcome inner obstacles. All this is done so individuals may develop new capacities inside themselves.

For mentors to engage in these transformational roles there is no need that they be significantly more expert than our sample individual. Basically, all are learning together. Just as kids in a sand pit are all at the same level of physical and social skills and learn from each other, so in the adult world learning naturally arises out of individuals doing together.

In the case of our individual with the servant disposition, in addition to friends taking on a variety of mentor roles, there will also be a mentor in spirit, perhaps more than one, who is keeping an eye out over a sequence of lives. These mentors in spirit offer a corrective steer when it is needed, to nudge the individual back onto its life plan. They also offer support during the between life period when the identity is processing what happened in the previous life and is planning the next.

Incidentally, there are mentors who specialise in selecting next life conditions. But they do not perform that task for all of any identity's thousand or so lives. They assist with selecting a sequence of lives, then move on to allow others with different types of expertise to advise regarding a new series of opportunities.

Does this mean it is like being in a school, in which you have different teachers for different subjects, who change year by year? Yes, it is somewhat like this. Mentors are selected according to what is appropriate at the level the identity has reached. The difference between this and schools is that school teachers have classes of twenty to thirty, or more, and that inevitably means the teacher is an especially good fit for some students and an especially poor fit for others, with most students neutral. In contrast, spiritual mentors are selected for that one individual, and they work with that individual until the lessons are learned and that sequence of lives is completed. Whether the mentor then maintains the mentor relationship is newly evaluated and a decision for continued mentorship is made depending on what is required.

Another useful point that may be derived from this school analogy is that while students experience a change in their teachers, the school's senior staff remain the same. And they review each student's progress—or at least, ideally they do—ensuring that those who are struggling, or those who are learning faster than the others, have resources directed towards them that best assist their continued growth. On the spiritual level, there are similar overseeing mentors whose role is to keep an eye on a large group of identities and ensure that opportunities and interactions are directed their way as and when they need them. Trainee identities are not always aware of what these overseeing mentors are doing. They do catch occasional glimpses of their overseers, just as children catch glimpses of their school's principal on formal occasions or as they walk across the schoolyard. But, like school children, trainee identities are not privy to what is discussed about them. They learn that as and when it is required and appropriate.

From all this we see that mentorship is an important part of the learning process. You have mentors in each life. Some mentors are your good friends who you interact with over numerous lives. Others are more experienced individuals who have developed particular kinds of expertise that is appropriate to you now. You have overseeing mentors who work behind the scenes, helping you achieve your goals. And you play the role of mentor, whether for friends who need your help, or for others you don't know well for whom you have expertise they require.

Think of mentorship as an ever shifting mosaic of colours, in which everyone's colour changes as they evolve, to which everyone makes a unique and special contribution.

Question 21

What am I to the universe and its consciousness?

What can we all do, here and now, to help evolution? As an individual, what can I do? Do I contribute in any way to the collective consciousness of the universe? Do my individual thoughts make any contribution to the survival of the universe or impact on the Universal Consciousness? Is what I feel, think or do of any cosmic significance at all?

THE GUIDES RESPOND:

The universe was created some number of billions of years ago. Spiritual identities began exploring the reality in which they exist, and some discovered this physical universe. They discovered life blossoming in various parts of the universe as a natural outcome of the emergent forces that were embedded in the universe when it was created. In selected places conditions were subsequently manicured and physical species were groomed to facilitate the entry into them of spiritual identities.

The purpose for this is as we have repeatedly explained: physical existence offers an opportunity, a training opportunity to be exact, by which spiritual identities may test themselves, learn and grow.

As a result of the emergent forces in-built into the universe, under its own momentum it is evolving from a simpler state to a more complex state. Some scientists claim that the laws of inertia dictate that the universe will eventually run out of energy and suffer a heat death. That is, the universe's energy will become so dissipated that the universe will die. This is not so. While the physical universe is energetically isolated, and so no physical energy enters the universe from beyond it, at the same time various self-organising capacities are embedded in the universe, capacities that human scientists have not yet found, and so the universe's energy will not dissipate in the way some scientists claim. This means that the universe contains emergent qualities that have yet to flower into all their possible permutations and complexities.

Spiritual identities similarly evolve from a naive simple state to a much more experienced, nuanced and subtle state. As we have observed, when you, as a fragment, rejoin your fellow fragments and reunite into a reconstituted and much greater entity, the complexity of your awareness will grow exponentially. The richness of this complex unified awareness is beyond your ability to conceive or our ability to explain.

What this means for you now, in your current state, is that everything you do, feel and think, all the lessons you learn, the skills you develop, the insights you obtain, the knowledge you access, the understanding you develop, initially gets uploaded to your ongoing spiritual identity. So nothing you personally experience and learn is lost. It all contributes to your evolving identity as a spiritual fragment.

The upshot is that after you have lived a thousand lives, you are rich in experience. You are knowing, loving, hugely self-aware compared to your current embodied state, and you possess a wisdom born of hundreds upon hundreds of lives. This enriched state is inconceivable to you now. Every individual who has ever and will ever incarnate on this planet will become an unimaginably wiser individual than the best, bravest, most self-sacrificing person who has ever lived. You will be that broad and deep.

Then you will join all those who constitute your close family of fragments and, as a collective entity, your wisdom will become their wisdom, their wisdom will become your wisdom, and together you will increase your personal wisdom a thousand-fold.

You should gain comfort by knowing that in these two steps you directly contribute to the evolution initially of your own ongoing identity, then to the evolution of all your fellow travellers and explorers. What can you do to contribute to your own and others' evolution? Keep doing what you are already doing. The further you take things, the more you shed what holds you back, and the deeper you travel, it all makes a vital contribution.

So this is the first level of response to your question. The next level is, what does this contribute to the physical universe, and then to the collective consciousness behind all?

As far as the physical universe goes, whenever you progress a skill or develop expertise, each time you perfect a movement, generate love towards others, and progress a line of thinking, you add to what could be called the human cultural stream. This stream exists in parallel to the physical, material universe, in close association with it. In a sense, the cultural stream embodies all humanity's higher accomplishments. This stream becomes available to anyone who lifts themselves to an inner level sufficient to enable them to draw on it.

One direct impact of this cultural stream is that when a discovery is made by one person, it is added to the stream and others can then rapidly reach up and draw the same discovery from the stream. One individual's contribution helps lift everyone else.

Of course, that individual didn't work in a vacuum. He or she drew on the discoveries of those who went before them. So while an individual may push ahead and be the first to reach something new, in reality it is a collective effort in which advanced explorers are followed closely by those who consolidate the advance and prepare the ground for the next major progression.

Highly visible explorers, scientists, artists, technological innovators, and so on, make breakthroughs that add to the evolution of the cultural stream. But everyone does the same, just in smaller ways. That means everyone contributes in their own ways to the formation of humanity's cultural stream. Most individuals during a handful of lives make significant contributions. So what you personally do does contribute to the evolution of the universe. It is just that, naturally, human contributions are largely confined to this tiny corner of the universe.

The exception is when the cultural stream grows sufficiently that it may become a source of experience-based knowledge for those living in other cultures elsewhere in the universe. At this stage those capable of accessing such a cultural stream are already further advanced than humanity, so it remains untapped by anyone beyond the immediately human. But over the millennia, as it expands, it will offer a significant experiential field of knowledge, feeling and wisdom.

The question might be asked, what of other cultural streams generated by other physically incarnated spiritual species? Can human beings tap into them? Yes, they do exist. And yes, those engaged in between life processing sometimes do tap into those other cultural streams in order to develop their experience and knowledge.

In stating this we are not referring to some kind of library. There is an ancient tradition, related in Theosophical circles, that refers to the Akashic records. A notion has grown around this phrase that this is some kind of library full of tomes containing great wisdom. This library must be considered to be a metaphor only. In fact, a stream that you enter is much closer to the reality than the metaphor of a library. This is because accessing cultural streams is not a matter of reading or intellectually absorbing something. The process is more akin to immersing yourself in a particular experience, just as you would jump bodily into a deep stream.

To return to the question, the barriers you personally break through, the issues you resolve, and the advances you make in your life, all contribute to humanity's cultural stream. They therefore contribute to everyone's advancement. Those who follow you will start from that much higher a cultural point, or at least, they will find they reach it more easily. Has the path been broken for them? Not quite. They still have to make their own effort, as always, and develop the skills and sensitivity by which they may access any form of information. But progressively more resources will be available for them to tap into. All the innumerable cultural streams generated throughout the multiverse perform a similar function.

Hence just as human life and culture has become more complex as a result of the efforts incarnated individuals have made, gaining breadth, depth and subtlety, and just as this physical place called Earth has evolved physically and culturally, so have billions of other physical places throughout the universe evolved physically and culturally. In some places, cultural streams have merged. In this way the universe itself is evolving.

We are aware that in stating all this we have not discussed how the physical and the spiritual are connected. We have already discussed this at length and in some technical detail elsewhere, particularly in *The Matapaua Conversations* and *The Kosmic Web*. We won't repeat those points here. However, we will say that there is a much closer alignment of the physical and spiritual than human beings can conceive, let alone accept. We have been at pains to indicate the ways that you, in your own identity, shape, select and contribute to the circumstances of your life. This is an example of the spiritual, which is you in your ongoing spiritual identity, contributing to the development of physical circumstances.

We also note that human culture itself is formed by, and comes out of, the activities of incarnated spiritual identities. Animals don't need culture. Animals don't need elaborate sports games, or manicured gardens, or the Sistine Chapel. Animals only need to eat, procreate, find shelter when required, and sleep. That's it. Why do human beings do so much more than they need do as animals? It is because the spiritual part of them wants to explore, achieve, create, understand ... then do it all again, until whatever it is is the best it can be.

This drive to make the most and best of what you do is a spiritual drive. It is a manifestation of your intent as a spiritual identity. It contributes to the collective entity of which you are a part. And when you and your fellow fragments rejoin and reform your collective entity, you will sail off to other parts of reality where you will further explore, refine and develop. You will continue evolving into higher states and joining even greater entities.

Eventually, an indescribable moment in the timeless future, everything you collectively experience will be returned to the undifferentiated consciousness that creates everything and from which everything derives. What we all experience, learn and come to understand, all our knowledge, love and wisdom, will be passed back to that from which we have all come.

So would the universe and the source of all carry on as they are if any of us were not here? The answer is, yes, both the universe and the undifferentiated consciousness would carry on. So are we of any significance now we *are* here? Yes, absolutely. We are directly contributing, through our efforts, to the evolution of what, for want of a better word, we could call Reality. In this way all living creatures, from the tiniest amoeba to the most magnificent sentient creature, contribute to their own personal evolution, to the evolution of their species, and to the evolution of the universe they inhabit. And the spiritual identities that occupy those living physical creatures directly enhance the evolution of themselves, of their own greater entity, and of whatever that greater entity is part of, all the way up in scale to include the absolute fullness that reality encompasses.

In this sense, existence is simultaneously impersonal and personal. It doesn't need to be us. But it does have to be someone. As it has turned out, we're all here. We're all doing it. Together. With verve, enthusiasm and joy!

The transitory nature of truths

THE GUIDES SAY:

We hope this window onto reality offers you some insight into the wider perspective that we possess courtesy of the fact we dwell "up here" and can see the entire forest you live within, whereas you see only those trees that immediately surround you. Our responses are designed as an introductory set of talks that provide glimpses of the forest. We will continue this introductory approach in an ongoing series of short books such as this. The next will deal with issues around meditation.

Please appreciate that we use a great many metaphors. Much needs to be appreciated not literally, but in a sideways fashion, because what we are introducing largely exists outside your everyday frames of reference. We have attempted to normalise and make accessible things that are neither normal nor accessible to you in your everyday self. Explanations have necessarily been kept brief in order to provide succinct intelligible reading. Greater detail on many of the points raised is available in other publications.

In offering you wider glimpses of the forest it could be thought that we are opposing "our truth" to "your truth." The fact is, you have your truths, derived from what you have perceived and experienced, and we have our truths, derived from what we perceive and experience. Are anyone's truths full and complete? No. Our truths are adjusted as new experiences arrive. Old explanations, that made sense when we had one set of data, naturally fall away when new data arrives. In the course of processing what we offer here, you will need to evaluate your truths while remembering that truths wear out over time. As new discoveries are made previously established explanations, theories, dogmas, and expectations naturally lose their relevance.

We don't ask, much less do we demand, that you give up your truths just at our say so. Everyone has their own pace of learning, of shucking off the old and absorbing the new. The metaphor of the butterfly emerging from the chrysalis is appropriate here, to symbolise the fact that truths serve the important function of protecting you in a world that is decidedly rough and tumble. Projected, adopted and found truths provide a sanctuary within which you may huddle and feel yourself safe while dealing with life's vicissitudes. But all sanctuaries are temporary. Much else is out there waiting your engagement.

As you journey life by life, you build up a protective shield of truths many, many times. And each time you will emerge from that protective shield, just like a butterfly emerges from its chrysalis, and fly off into new roles, new opportunities, new realities. There, needing shelter, you will adopt ever new explanations, new truths—which you will cast off when you fly away once again.

So take on board whatever appeals to you here. Make use of whatever you find useful in your search for truths that more fully contextualise what you experience and perceive. Let go of old truths that are no longer relevant. There is no requirement to hold onto them, nor any stigma in letting them go. They have served their purpose. Release them, watch them fall away, and move on.

Until we meet again, we wish you well in your explorations. Beat back your fears. Trust your inner voice. Open yourself up to all you could be. A future "you" waits over the horizon. A "you" that you are creating each moment, with everything you feel, think, choose and do.

Do you want to learn more?

Are you interested in learning more about the guides' perspective on humanity's spiritual nature and development? A number of avenues are available for your further exploration.

Peter Calvert has archived all the material he has channelled since 1998. This is available at: wisdomschool.nz. In addition, on the website www.experimentalspirituality.net the guides offer observations on a range of topics.

Peter Clavert and Keith Hill have produced eleven channelled books—and counting. Initiated by the guides, these books offer a generally consistent approach to individual spiritual development. Regarding these books, the guides state:

Many aspects of human life and spirituality are presented, some with no apparent connection to other aspects. A wide scope is required because what is termed spiritual development—which is actually the process of you as a seeker expanding your awareness so it is not dominated by coarse body level impressions but becomes open to numerous kinds of subtle perceptions and ways of knowing—is a multifacted and very complex task.

Some of the materials we and others have generated will mean nothing to one person, yet to another it provides an ah-ha! revelation. We seek to serve all people, at all stages of progress, as they encounter many very different varieties of experiences. Practically no one who has ever lived has been what might be called "the complete package." One person knows in depth what another is not even aware of. And vice versa. This is inevitable, given the subtle complexities that human life offers. Most are barely scratching the surface. And we include those who have honed their expertise in arcane areas of human existence. We seek to be expansive in the scope of materials we offer in order to provide everyone who is interested with information that will add to their knowledge of what they are undergoing. It is a natural outcome of this intent that the material on offer will strike different people with different levels of intensity. Some material will light a fire within. Other material will inevitably leave you cold.

Accordingly, we advise those who wish to explore the texts we have initiated to initially follow up what attracts you and what resonates with you. However, there is always a corresponding need to dig deeper into motives. So you also need to become aware of which part of you is attracted and begun resonating. Is it your deepest self? Or is it that you wish to act in accordance with what another person, who you respect, has said? Or with what you think you need? Is the issue you are exploring taking you deeper? Or is it keeping you at the same level? Are you learning things you didn't know? Or are you seeking to confirm what you already know? Or are you using an interest in a particular topic to push away a nagging issue you know, deep down, is what really has to be addressed?

These questions need to be asked. If you establish an ongoing relationship with us, these are the questions with which we will confront you. We promote a level of discomfort, because discomfort is always involved in self-transformation. It is only by challenging what you are and know now that you can expand your awareness and become and know more than you currently do. Note that discomfort in this sense is a transitory part of a larger process. Discomfort is not a goal or desired in and of itself.

Clearly, everyone needs to put a toe into the water before they can decide whether jumping in is for them. Please feel free to explore the texts on offer at your leisure. And we look forward to learning more about one another some time in the future.

The books produced to date are as follow:

THE CHANNELLED Q+A SERIES

This series presents easy-to-read, non-technical books that explore spirituality at an introductory level. For each, the guides set a general topic for discussion, then had Keith Hill, this series' channeller, invite people he knew to submit questions, which the guides then answered. Each book contains twenty-one questions and answers, with a number of questions picking up and expanding on prior answers. The result is a spontaneous to-and-fro in which, as the guides comment, many surprising and unanticipated topics are explored. On the other hand, the guides also surprise with their answers. As of this publication there are three books in this series. While they are listed in the sequence they were created, they are designed to be read as stand-alone texts, and in any order.

What Is Really Going On?
The first in this series focuses on reincarnation and its implications, along with a range of key spiritual topics.

Where Do I Go When I Meditate?
The guides discuss not just the possibilities that meditation creates, but also chakras, prayer, what we gain from entering the spiritual realm, and the nature of extra-terrestrials.

How Did I End Up Here?
This book addresses life plans, diet, allergies and autism, personal development and introduce the process of self-enquiry.

THE CHANNELLED SPIRITUALITY SERIES

This series is designed for those who wish to engage in personal psychospiritual development. It provides a means for seekers to understand their individual psychospiritual make-up, what factors drive their current existence, and what the key factors of their life plan involve. In this sense, the Channelled Spirituality Series offers a practical way to carry out self-enquiry.

The series' channeller, Keith Hill, has a background in the Fourth Way Work teaching of G.I. Gurdjieff. Because these books have been offered through Keith's mind, they build on what he understands of the Gurdjieff Work. In addition, Keith has been directed to the Michael Teachings. These were originally channelled by a group in San Francisco, who had also been trained in the Gurdjieff Work. The Michael Teachings add many details to the Gurdjieff Work, the most fundamental being that it puts psychospiritual development into a reincarnational context. The Michael Teachings also add considerably to Gurdjieff's ideas on human psychological make-up.

Selections from all this material have been utilised by the guides in the Channelled Spirituality Series to create a straightforward, psychologically-based approach to personal spiritual development.

Experimental Spirituality

Introduces the rationale for adopting a non-religious, empirical and experimental approach to spirituality. Key concepts include the journey from belief to knowledge, how human identity is structured, the nature of the five-layered self, and how developing understanding relies on asking questions in the right way.

Practical Spirituality

Considers the psychospiritual factors we draw on when planning each incarnation. Topics include examining reincarnation and its impact on evolving identity, the rationale behind life plans, the nature and purpose of karma, confronting negativities and nurturing positive qualities within, and the role of life lessons in helping us mature.

Psychological Spirituality

Uses the paired concepts of true and false personality to explore how human identity is formed and plays out during the course of a life. This book also considers how lives are linked into sequences that form a unique trajectory through the human world, and what it takes to initiate self-transformation.

METAPHYSICS FOR THE TWENTY-FIRST CENTURY
— Channelled by Peter Calvert and Keith Hill

Metaphysical descriptions map the unknown terrain that surrounds us. Historically, religions have supplied humanity's metaphysical descriptions of reality. But today they have become outmoded. We need new metaphysical descriptions that chime with current knowledge. Such descriptions are offered in the following books.

The Kosmic Web

Begins at the beginning, with the creation of the multiverse, then discusses the seeding of ecosystems, biological life and humanity. To do so, the book refreshes ancient concepts using new terminology: the nature of Dao, the nature of the electrospiritual, the function of the aura, and the evolution of nodes and node fragments. *The Kosmic Web* is recommended as the primary text for appreciating the guides' view of existence.

The Matapaua Conversations

This book is Peter and Keith's first presentation. Keith asked the guides one hundred "big" questions regarding the big bang, evolution, the nature of consciousness, and other related metaphysical topics. Peter then took time out at Matapaua Beach to receive the answers, keeping a diary to record his experiences and thoughts throughout. This book complements the material presented in *The Kosmic Web*.

Learning Who You Are

Drawing on a variety of texts, including Peter's extensive archive of channelled material, this book offers an easy-to-read overview of the guides' outlook. This is an ideal introduction to the guides' outlook.

CHANNELLED BY PETER CALVERT

Guided Healing

This book contains two urgent messages. To spiritual seekers, *Guided Healing* presents a novel view of the spiritual purpose and benefits of being born into a physical body. Issues covered include the relationship between the spiritual and physical realms, the reason for incarnation, the use of meditation as a means for exploring the spiritual realm, and the significance of soul work.

To healers, *Guided Healing* offers instruction on how to become a conduit for healing energy that emanates from the spiritual realm. Topics covered include how to contact guides in the spiritual realm, the nature of spiritual perception, and factors which enhance or hinder energy flow during the act of healing.

Agape and the Hierarchy of Love

After years of meditating, Peter Calvert found himself communicating with non-embodied beings. These beings gave him metaphysical and personal training in what they called "spiritual empiricism". This book is a commendium of these messages. It includes numerous models that illustrate the relationship of the physical and spiritual domains.

All books may be purchased at your favourite store. To learn more and to read chapter excerpts go to www.attarbooks.com.

To the reader

Small presses rely on the support of readers to tell others about the books they enjoy. To support this book and its author, we ask you to consider placing a review on the site where you bought it. For more on Keith Hill and his books, and for free ebooks, go to his author website, www.keithhillauthor.com. Other books written by Keith Hill on spiritual topics are:

The Bhagavad Gita: A new poetic translation

"An enthralling new rendering of a classic text that achieves the rare feat of balancing spiritual insight, poetic power and philosophic accuracy". — Peter Calvert, co-author of *The Kosmic Web*

Written in poetry, but usually rendered into prose, this version balances the need to present the *Bhagavad Gita's* profound concepts precisely while reproducing the original poem's dramatic and poetic power. This translation is especially successful in capturing the *Bhagavad Gita's* shifts of tone, moving from vivid descriptions of the battlefield, to the precise reasoning of Krishna's advice to Arjuna, to the sublime visionary intensity of Krishna as cosmic being. Endnotes and a glossary help readers unfamiliar with Indian culture understand the poem's mythological and philosophic references.

The Ecstasy of Cabeza de Vaca

""A tour de force ... impossible to put down." – Alistair Paterson

"An extraordinary effort of imagination. In New Zealand literature there's no one quite like Keith Hill, and certainly no long poem like this one." —Roger Horrocks

In 1528, a Spanish expedition was shipwrecked in the Gulf of Mexico. Eight years later only four men remained alive. One of the four, Cabeza de Vaca, later published an account of what occurred. Naked and enslaved, de Vaca was stripped of all he possessed, then underwent an extraordinary transformation. *The Ecstasy of Cabeza de Vaca* is Keith Hill's masterful retelling of Cabeza de Vaca's story. This is a heartbreaking account of courage and faith, barbarity and miracles, that transports us to the limits of human experience.

Interpretations of Desire: Mystical love poems by the Sufi Master Ibn 'Arabi

"Keith Hill's artful and beautiful renditions will bring Ibn 'Arabi's neglected masterpiece to a new readership."—Nile Green, author of *Sufism: A Global History*

In 1201, Ibn 'Arabi arrived in Mecca. Among those who impressed him was Nizám, the daughter of a prominent religious teacher. As Beatrice did for Dante, Nizám soon inspired a sequence of love poems that are Ibn 'Arabi's masterpiece, *Tarjumán al-Aswáq*. This collection reveals that with his intense feeling, vivid imagery, and the playful way he reworked the conventions of Bedouin desert poetry, Ibn 'Arabi's love poems are among the best in all Sufi literature.

I Cannot Live Without You: Selected poems of Mirabai and Kabir

"Reminded me it's been an eternity since I was hungry for God. This book will renew your hunger for your sacred flame." —Judith Hoch PhD, author of *Prophecy on the River*

Mirabai and Kabir are among India's greatest mystic poets. These vivid contemporary versions reflect the original poetic forms, and penetrate to the heart of their spiritual passion.

Psalms of Exile and Return

"In a time that is spiritually dry for so many, this book of psalms is water in the desert. They challenge, terrify, comfort, and call us to a deep humanity." Allan Jones, Dean Emeritus, Grace Cathedral, San Francisco

In 587 BCE, King Zedekiah of Judah led his people in rebellion against Babylonian rule. Nebuchadnezzar responded mercilessly. His army sacked Jerusalem, destroyed the Temple, and deported thousands to Babylon. These psalms are written from the perspective of one of those exiles, recounting his growing despair in Babylon, his escape and reuniting with his lost beloved, and their return to Jerusalem.

NON-FICTION

The God Revolution

Winner, Best Book 2011 Ashton Wylie Awards

"An impressive and accessible introduction to a challenging philosophical topic." —Kirkus Review
"Deserves to be read by all those who care about ideas, the trajectory of civilization and its future form." —Peter Dornauf, www.eyecontact.com

The God Revolution examines how the scientific revolution led to new insights into reality, that in turn led leading thinkers to propose new concepts of God. The result is a stimulating and ultimately inspiring journey, surveying pivotal moments in Western cultural and intellectual history, and revealing revolutionary new insights into the nature and role of God that continue to resonate in our lives today.

These books are available at your favourite online store or may be ordered through your local bookshop. To read chapter excerpts and find out more go to www.attarbooks.com.